Writing Strategies
for Social Studies

Author

Sarah Kartchner Clark, M.A.Ed.

SHELL EDUCATION

Editor
Conni Medina

Assistant Editor
Leslie Huber

Senior Editor
Lori Kamola, M.S.Ed.

Editor-in-Chief
Sharon Coan, M.S.Ed.

Editorial Manager
Gisela Lee, M.A.

Creative Director
Lee Aucoin

Cover Design
Lee Aucoin

Illustrator
Karen M. Lowe

Imaging
Robin Erickson
Phil Garcia
Don Tran

Publisher
Corinne Burton, M.A.Ed.

Shell Education
5301 Oceanus Drive
Huntington Beach, CA 92649-1030
http://www.shelleducation.com
ISBN 978-1-4258-0058-1
©2007 Shell Educational Publishing, Inc.
Reprinted 2011

WTP 3791

Table of Contents

Introduction

Part 1: Writing to Learn in Social Studies

Part 2: Writing to Apply in Social Studies

Part 3: Assessment

Introduction:
Writing Across the Curriculum

What Is Writing?

For thousands of years, humans have been communicating by writing down characters, symbols, numbers, or letters with implied meaning. Being able to write and to write well is more important today than ever before. According to *http://www.dictionary.com*, the definition of writing is the making of letters or characters that constitute readable matter with the intent to convey meaning. Writing demands that one not only know how to read what one has written, but also know the rules of writing that dictate how characters or letters are to be written and therefore understood.

What is writing? Is it brainstorming? Is it spelling? Is it scribbling words and phrases? Is it a report? Is it a simple paragraph? Writing in the classroom can be simply defined as any symbolic representation (Hefflin and Hartman 2002). As Hefflin and Hartman (2002) explain, the definition of writing includes representations that are "linguistic, graphic, pictorial, or otherwise." This broad definition of writing welcomes a variety of writing formats.

Because educators understand the need for improved reading and writing skills in students, there has been a renewed focus on teaching literacy skills over the past several decades. This emphasis and focus, however, has not yielded the desired results. The number of students graduating from high school without the literacy skills needed to thrive in a global community continues to increase (Fisher and Ivey 2005). National attention has been refocused on the literacy needs of students, but so far this emphasis has been on the importance of reading and writing in language arts, and it has not affected the content areas. The focus on literacy has not changed the way that content areas are taught (e.g. Lesley 2005; O'Brien, Stewart, and Moje 1995; O'Brien and Stewart 1989). There is still much work to be done in the area of reading, writing, and comprehension in the content areas.

Most educators agree on the need for writing instruction in the content areas but differ on where instruction should occur. Because of curriculum demands, many teachers feel there is not enough time to teach writing in the content areas; adding one more component is just too much strain on the time and quality of lessons. However, researchers claim that most writing assignments do not need to be graded, which eliminates a major concern about the teacher workload (Worsley and Mayer 1989; Hightshue 1988; Self 1987).

Writing is powerful. Writing is an instrument of thinking that allows students to express their thoughts. Writing helps students understand and share their perceptions of the world around them. Teachers can give students power in their world by teaching them to write and to write well. The written word ". . . enables the writer, perhaps for the first time, to sense the power of . . . language to affect another. Through using, selecting and rejecting, arranging and rearranging language, the student comes to understand how language is used" (Greenberg and Rath 1985, p. 12).

Introduction:
Writing Across the Curriculum *(cont.)*

Writing Across the Curriculum

Social Studies teachers may wonder where writing fits in the social studies curriculum. What do run-on sentences have to do with forms of government and geography? The answer lies in the fact that writing is the means through which students are able to articulate complex terms and synthesize concepts. Writing is a tool that students can use to understand and dissect the subject of social studies. Writing is a tool that allows students to translate complex ideas into words and language that they understand.

There is an overemphasis on the process of writing instead of using writing to assist comprehension and understanding (Fisher and Frey 2004). In general, writing assignments in social studies mainly consist of asking students to write the answers to the questions at the end of the textbook chapter, with an occasional formal social studies report or research report required with little direction from the teacher. Evidence shows social studies achievement increases when students are actively engaged in reading, thinking, and writing about what they are learning.

Research shows that there are two forms of writing that need to take place across all subject matters being taught. One form is called writing to learn, and the other form is learning to write. Anne Walker (1988) explains that the two forms are parts of a virtual circle. Writing allows students to become active in their learning. Active learning requires active thinking. In order to write, students need to be actively thinking (Steffens 1988; Walker 1988). A teacher who works as a facilitator of knowledge will encourage deeper thinking, therefore increasing student understanding (Self 1987; Hamilton-Wieler 1988).

Does Writing Across the Curriculum Work?

Research studies (Gere 1985; Barr and Healy 1988) seem to suggest that writing in the content areas does make a difference. Barr and Healy (1988) state that "schools succeed when the emphasis by both teachers and students is on writing and thinking about relevant and significant ideas within the subject areas." The encouragement of writing across the curriculum leads to higher-order thinking skills (Gere 1985). Shifts in student attitudes have also been documented as a great benefit to writing across the curriculum (Winchester 1987).

Is there enough time to write and cover all the objectives and demands of the social studies curriculum? Research shows that writing can help meet those objectives and demands. Here are three time-saving advantages to consider (Worsley and Mayer 1989; Hightshue 1988; Self 1987):

- Social studies teachers find that they need less review time if students write about the concepts.

- Social studies teachers spend less time reteaching content after testing if they have incorporated writing strategies in the curriculum.

- Most writing in social studies classrooms does not need to be heavily graded, so the teacher's workload is decreased.

Introduction:
Writing Across the Curriculum *(cont.)*

The Reading/Writing Connection

According to Gay Su Pinnell in the article "Success of Children at Risk in a Program That Combines Writing and Reading," "As children read and write they make the connections that form their basic understandings about both. Learning in one area enhances learning in the other. There is ample evidence to suggest that the processes are inseparable and that we should examine pedagogy in the light of these interrelationships. Hence, the two activities should be integrated in instructional settings. Teachers need to create supportive situations in which children have opportunities to explore the whole range of literacy learning, and they need to design instruction that helps children make connections between reading and writing."

Writing is the expression of ideas and thoughts gathered while reading. Social Studies texts are often heavily loaded with difficult vocabulary words and complex concepts that are challenging for students to understand. Encouraging students to both read and write helps them understand the information presented. When students read content without writing about it, they miss a crucial step in the process of understanding the information.

Ideas and Questions to Consider

The emphasis on literacy is not enough. The new emphasis is on *content literacy* (Fisher and Ivey 2005). Content literacy supports the view that students construct knowledge through activities such as reading, discussion, and writing. Students must begin to personally connect with the content information they are learning and gathering as they study social studies.

Fisher and Frey (2004) explain that learning is language-based. Telling students information is not sufficient. Students must think about, read about, talk about, and write about information in order to synthesize it and to retain it. Reading and writing are critical to all learning. Questions to ask about how to incorporate reading and writing into content area learning are suggested by Hefflin and Hartman (2002):

- How do you determine what to write about?

- What is the goal and the purpose of the writing?

- How will the writing be assessed?

- What is being activated or constructed by the writing?

- What supports the bridge between what the students write and read?

- Who does the writing in social studies class?

- What role does discussion play in preparing to write?

- What role does discussion play during writing?

- How will you know the writing activity or assignment is successful?

- How will you know when to use which writing strategy?

Introduction:
Writing Across the Curriculum *(cont.)*

Writing to Learn

Writing helps create the bridge between the content knowledge and understanding. Reading from the textbook and answering the questions is a very passive way to learn. A wide variety of writing assignments and activities can help students become actively engaged in social studies. Examples include social studies observation journals, free writes, vocabulary journals, observation reports, topic analyses, diagrams, and charts. All of these writing formats encourage students to think about social studies and connect prior knowledge or experiences with new learning.

Writing to learn is expressive writing that encourages students to write about what they are thinking and learning. Examples of this type of writing are journal entries, reflections, reading responses, question-answering, personal notations, etc.

Not all writing-to-learn activities must be graded. Teachers should offer feedback and comments but should not feel compelled to grade the spelling, grammar, organization, and content of these writing activities. The purpose of writing-to-learn activities is to promote active learning, encourage discussion, engage all students, and encourage thinking. There is usually a required time set aside to complete the writing. These less formal writing assignments may be expanded into more formal assignments.

Writing to Apply

When students use their new knowledge in social studies to write in a more formal manner, they are writing to apply. In these activities, students are asked to analyze and synthesize information, and then communicate their thoughts in a coherent, organized manner. This type of writing can be more challenging for students because they need to not only understand the content and be able to process it at a higher level, but also communicate it using the strategies of the writing process, the features of the chosen genre, and the conventions of the grade level. Teachers are most likely comfortable with this type of writing in social studies class, as it may have been what they were exposed to in school.

Some familiar examples of this type of writing are social studies lab reports and research reports. However, there are many other options to consider: microthemes, friendly letters, business letters, social studies fiction stories, and more.

Unlike writing-to-learn activities, writing-to-apply activities are meant to be graded. With these assignments, students are showing what they have learned and demonstrating the capability to communicate it in a formal writing format. A variety of assessment options are described in Part 3 of this book.

Introduction: Motivating Students to Write

Social Studies Library

One of the easiest and most effective ways to improve literacy is to allow time for students to read during class. Students who frequently read a wide variety of materials have better vocabularies and better reading comprehension skills. As Ryder and Graves (2003) point out, wide reading fosters automaticity in students because it exposes them to more words in different contexts, provides them with knowledge on a variety of topics, and promotes life-long reading habits. Teachers can create a social studies library corner by collecting and providing books for students to read. Social Studies teachers have an intimate knowledge of social studies-based reading materials for a wide range of reading abilities, so they can recommend books to any student to read outside of class.

Lesley Mandel Morrow, president of the International Reading Association (2003–04), explains that research indicates children in classrooms with literature collections read 50 percent more books than children in classrooms without such collections. Work with the school librarian or media specialist to build and create a social studies library corner. There is a variety of reading materials available on these topics:

- communities (people in the community, jobs in the communities, places to visit, etc.)
- families and culture (family organization, traditions, culture, ways of living, etc.)
- United States history (colonial times, Revolutionary War, Civil War, westward expansion, Industrial Revolution, foreign wars, etc.)
- world history (ancient civilizations)
- biographies (Madame Curie, George Washington, Martin Luther King, Jr., George Washington Carver, Thomas Alva Edison, Harriet Tubman, etc.)

The Writing Process Center

The writing process involves the different stages from developing an idea to publishing a piece of written work. Students need support to create a finished product. Teachers can set up permanent stations throughout their classrooms for each stage of the writing process. This not only motivates students at each stage of the writing process but also makes it easier to incorporate all stages of the process. This way the students will have access to all the materials needed to work through the writing process. Here are some ideas for each station of the writing process:

- **prewriting** – books with writing suggestions and ideas, story starts, writing samples, pieces of writing about social studies, blank graphic organizers, books and magazines about social studies topics, and encyclopedias

- **drafting** – established rubrics and criteria, music available for students who need a relaxing environment as they write, resources, pencils, erasers, floor pillows, and comfortable places to sit and write

- **revising** – peer editing checklists, samples of quality writing, rubrics, word lists (such as a list of vivid verbs to replace more overly used verbs), etc.

- **editing** – dictionaries, thesauruses, writing reference books, colored pens or pencils, and proofreading checklists

- **publishing** – computers, pens, bookbinding materials, sample finished products, a printer, colored pencils for illustrations and diagrams, rulers, and a variety of lined and unlined paper

Introduction:
Motivating Students to Write *(cont.)*

Spotlight Reading

Set aside a time each week for students to read aloud and share the writing they have accomplished. These writings may be less formal pieces such as journals, free writes, or feature analyses, or they may be formal writing pieces like observation reports or social studies experiment reports. This practice keeps students focused and aware of an audience as they write, and it allows them the opportunity to give and receive feedback. It is an effective way to validate the hard work and effort of students and may even eliminate the need for the teacher to formally assess a piece of writing. Finally, this spotlight reading also provides an opportunity for students to hear their writing aloud. They will automatically think of things they are learning about social studies objectives and they will become more aware of what they need to change to improve their writing.

Bulletin Board Writing Display

Student exposure to writing is often limited. Therefore it is imperative for the teacher to provide students with a wide variety of writing samples relating to social studies (Ryder and Graves 2003). These samples should be available for students to look at and use as models. Designate a bulletin board in the classroom to display these writing samples. Be sure to add to the collection frequently so that students remain interested and curious about the new additions. Encourage students to bring in samples of writing that are related to social studies. This will also help them locate and identify writing samples related to social studies.

Introduction:
The Writing Process

"A writer," says Britton, "draws on the whole store of his experience, and his whole social being, so that in the act of writing he imposes his own individuality" (1975, p. 47). The most complex form of writing is the college-level argumentative essay. Taking notes is the least complex form of writing. Writing for meaning and expressing oneself to others is intricate and complex work. Using the writing process helps the writer take a piece of writing from the beginning, or brainstorming, to the end, or the published piece. This process is especially important to follow as students write reports and other social studies writing assignments. The writing process at the emergent writing level is usually conducted as a group, though on occasion it is done individually. Students in higher grades who have more familiarity with the writing process can complete it individually.

What is the writing process? It includes prewriting, drafting, editing/revising, publishing, and reflection. Read the description of the writing process steps below. There are different points to consider at each step of the writing process.

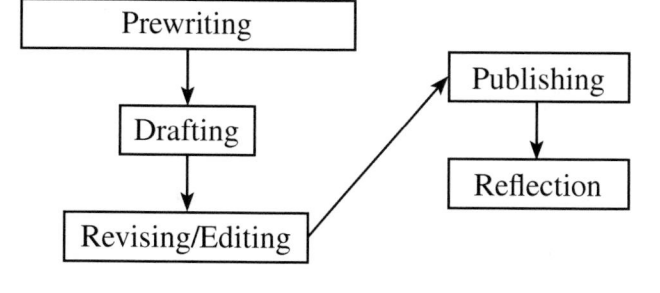

Prewriting

This is the phase where all writing begins. At this stage, writers generate ideas, brainstorm topics, web ideas together, or talk or think about ideas. Teachers explain that students may get writing ideas from personal experiences, stories, pictures, magazines, newspapers, television, and a variety of other sources.

This phase sets the foundation for a specific piece of writing. Before brainstorming or prewriting can begin, students need instruction on the genre or format (lab report, journal entry, visual presentation, etc.), audience (the teacher, fellow classmates, social studies competition judges, etc.), and purpose (to explain, to persuade, to inform, etc.). These elements impact the types of information to brainstorm.

Students need to have a clear understanding of a social studies topic before they are expected to write or report on it. Teachers can provide resources for research and model note-taking strategies. Social Studies topics are often complex and difficult to understand, so discussion will help prepare students to write. Note-taking (pages 99–107) and diagram and mapping strategies (pages 108–139) can help students organize the major points in their writing.

What does prewriting look like?

- researching a chosen topic
- analyzing the characteristics of the intended genre
- examining sample writing pieces
- discussing the topic with the teacher, a partner, or the class
- brainstorming ideas about the topic
- using webbing or other graphics to organize information
- discussing the assessment tool

Introduction:
The Writing Process *(cont.)*

Drafting

At the drafting stage of the writing process, students begin to put their ideas on paper. Students need to keep in mind the genre or format, audience, and purpose. For beginning writers, pictures and drawings may very well be part of the composition. Teachers should encourage students to write as much as they can on their own throughout the writing process.

Another area that students struggle with is writing in an orderly manner. Students should already have graphic organizers, notes, or outlines from the prewriting stage that can help them sequence and organize their writing.

What does drafting look like?

- working fairly quickly
- leaving blank spaces for missing words
- guessing at spelling
- focusing on simply putting ideas on paper
- using notes or graphic organizers to stay focused
- drafting a preliminary version of the writing assignment (story, letter, report, essay, etc.)

Revising and Editing

This phase of writing consists of two parts: revision looks at the organization and the structure of the writing, while editing looks at the mechanics of the writing. Students must understand how to do both. When revising, students analyze their writing for the required traits: sequencing words in a lab report, descriptive language in a social studies fiction story, topic sentences and supporting details in a persuasive essay. They also ask questions of their writing: *Does it make sense? Is anything out of order? Should anything be added or deleted?* Use the Self-Assessment Survey (pages 194–195) to give students an opportunity to evaluate their own writing. Individual Teacher Conferences (pages 198–199) are also helpful to give students feedback throughout the writing process.

What does revising and editing look like?

- reading the writing aloud to make sure that it makes sense
- adding missing information
- deleting unnecessary, incorrect, or duplicate information
- proofreading for spelling, capitalization, grammar, and punctuation
- self-analysis by students
- conferences with peers or the teacher

Introduction:
The Writing Process *(cont.)*

Publishing

Publishing allows students to celebrate their hard work. It occurs after the other steps are completed and the student is ready to produce the final copy, which can be handwritten or typed on a word processor. Teachers should consider the abilities of their students. The goal is to present the written information attractively, so others can enjoy it.

What does publishing look like?

- creating a final copy
- adding illustrations, borders, a cover, etc.
- sharing orally
- publishing "in-house" in a class book
- posting on a classroom bulletin board

Reflecting

Reflection is a key element in the writing process. It encourages the writer to think about his or her writing, look at the writing from a different point of view, and see progress in writing effort. Reflection also allows the writer to look back at brainstorming and the beginning of a writing project to see if the original goals were met.

What does reflection look like?

- Reading what has been written and asking the following questions:
  Is that what I wanted to say?
  Is there more I should have written?
  Which is my favorite part in this writing?
  Did I write this piece the way I planned to?
  What can I learn from this assignment?
  How can I continue to improve my writing?

Differentiating Instruction

For ELLs, teachers need to modify writing assignments and rubrics to fit students' individual language proficiencies. They will benefit from preteaching and frequent review and application of new vocabulary, so that they can incorporate those words into their writing. Also, teachers can provide scaffolding by way of graphic organizers for teaching content and developing and organizing their thoughts during the prewriting phase. Sentence or paragraph frames can help these students express their ideas in a more coherent manner when they begin drafting their writing. Frequent writing conferences can help the teacher assess learning and identify needs.

Students who are reading or writing below grade level will benefit from scaffolding as well. They may need to be constantly reminded to refer to their rubric—which should be adapted to address their individual needs—to meet the expectations of the assignment. Teachers can provide graphic organizers during the prewriting phase to help these students get started in an organized fashion. When revising and editing, teachers can model how to identify errors and make changes so that these students have a clear understanding of this difficult stage of the writing process.

Gifted students can be challenged at each step of the writing process to work more independently, create longer or more elaborate pieces, use multiple sources, write from a different point of view, incorporate richer vocabulary, or write with a greater variety of sentence structures. Teachers should also adapt rubrics to challenge these students.

Introduction: Writing Instruction

What Great Teachers Do to Encourage Writing in Social Studies

1. **Share vocabulary-rich books and reading materials about the subjects you are studying in social studies class.** Sloan (1996) explains that the best source of learning about social studies vocabulary is reading good books that use the words. This allows the teacher to introduce them, allows the opportunity for students to hear them in context, and provides an opportunity to discuss the social studies vocabulary words.

2. **Provide plenty of time for students to experience the writing process** (Corona, Spangenberger, and Venet 1998). It takes time to teach the writing process, but it is worth it. Taking a writing project from planning to publication is very meaningful to students because it validates their efforts and understanding of social studies concepts.

3. **Allow time for students to evaluate others' writing and receive teacher feedback** (Corona, Spangenberger, and Venet 1998). Writing is communication. Students need to share their writing with others, both giving and receiving feedback from peers and teachers. This helps to cement students' understanding of social studies concepts. The process also provides teachers with the opportunity to clarify and reteach concepts as needed.

4. **Offer daily writing opportunities to your students.** "A writer-centered classroom emphasizes using written expression to communicate ideas. Writing is an important part of all areas of the curriculum" (Corona, Spangenberger, and Venet 1998, p. 29). Be sure to include a wide variety of assignments. Some assignments might be more formal while others may be more casual. Also include a range of different types of writing such as journal entries, outlines, poetry, reports, short stories, etc. Students usually benefit from having a choice about what they are to write about. Encourage students to use social studies vocabulary when they write.

5. **Encourage students to be aware of and look for new and interesting social studies words.** Students can just browse through books looking for words that catch their attention and add them to their vocabulary journals. They may also be assigned to look for specific social studies words that are being studied in class. Finally, create a Social Studies Word Wall in your classroom (see pages 21–24).

6. **Incorporate practice and repetition as a way for students to become familiar with vocabulary words and how they are to be used** (Laflamme 1997). Students can be exposed through writing, discussions, modeling, classroom exercises, and reading.

7. **Teach students the strategies to read, understand, and write about increasingly complex text.** These same strategies can help students work through difficult concepts to arrive at deep learning. Students who can recognize text patterns will be better prepared to use those patterns in their own writing (Fisher and Ivey 2005).

8. **Focus students' reading and writing on big ideas.** Don't get caught up in the details. Rote learning does not lend itself to lifelong learning. Focusing on themes, concepts, and big ideas lends itself to linking new information to prior knowledge as well as life experiences and events that are happening in the world today.

Introduction:
Writing Instruction *(cont.)*

Writing Venues in the Social Studies Classroom

Social Studies teachers can easily incorporate the same techniques that language arts teachers have used for years to help students become more strategic and skilled writers and to help them comprehend and write about the social studies materials they encounter. There are a variety of ways to teach students new ideas and to incorporate writing into the social studies curriculum. The first is to consider changing class configurations to use writing in social studies. Content-area teachers often lecture to the whole class and seldom pair students together or assign small groups to work together for reading and writing. Following are suggestions for the types of configurations a social studies teacher can consider:

Large groups are best for:

- introducing a new writing strategy
- modeling think-alouds to show how good writers work through a piece of writing
- practicing think-alouds to apply a strategy to students' own writing and allowing students to share their experiences and ideas using the strategy

Small groups are best for:

- providing more intensive instruction for students who need it
- introducing gifted students to a new writing piece or strategy so that they can apply it independently to more challenging writing assignments
- preteaching new strategies to ELLs or students who are below grade level
- preteaching new vocabulary to ELLs

Conferences are best for:

- checking a student's understanding of social studies concepts and the writing strategies being used
- providing intensive writing strategy instruction to a student who may need extra attention
- coaching a child in how he/she might reveal his/her thinking by writing to others
- pushing a child to use a strategy to think more deeply than he or she might have imagined possible
- individually editing and correcting student writing

Pair students with partners:

- to discuss free writes, dialogue journals, think-pair-share, etc.
- to edit and gather input on product writing pieces

Introduction:
Writing Instruction *(cont.)*

Habits of Highly Effective Writers

Duke and Pearson (2001) have established that good readers read and write a lot. They also set goals, make predictions, and read selectively. Many of the same practices of good readers are also done by good writers. Here are some more specific suggestions for highly effective writers:

- **Good writers write all the time.** The more experience one has writing, the better writer he or she becomes. Learning to write takes practice and more practice!

- **Good writers read a lot.** Reading provides a great model for writers as to what the finished product looks like (Fisher and Ivey 2005). Students who read will know how to write better than those who do not.

- **Good writers are aware of correct spelling.** There are no excuses for poor spelling. Commit to learning and using correct spelling in writing—even in the rough draft, if possible. Good writers use all the resources available and understand the limitations of computer spell-check programs.

- **Good writers appreciate critiques and feedback.** Good writers have a "thick skin" and ask for input and suggestions from many different sources.

- **Good writers keep a learning log handy.** The learning log can be used to store good writing ideas, to document what is being learned, to activate prior knowledge, and to question what is being learned (Brozo and Simpson 2003; Cwilka and Martinez-Cruz 2003; Fisher and Frey 2004). Using this learning log also helps cement learning and helps students avoid writer's block.

- **Good writers write for a variety of purposes.** Learning to write in a variety of formats makes for a well-rounded, experienced writer. Teachers should expose students to different types of social studies writing formats.

- **Good writers read and edit other people's writing.** Good writers look for opportunities to work with others to improve their writing. Peer editing groups are an excellent way to get feedback and reinforcement from peers. This feedback is important for the self-image of the writer (Gahn 1989). Editing others' work will also help students recognize writing errors, such as an off-topic response, a weak topic sentence, a lack of supporting detail, weak vocabulary, and errors in spelling or grammar.

- **Good writers think objectively.** Good writers need to be able to step back and really look at their writing. Some writers are so happy to be done with their writing that they never really look at it again.

- **Good writers read it out loud!** Teachers can encourage students to give their writing a voice. Many errors or additions are discovered when a student listens to the writing being read aloud.

- **Good writers use and create rubrics and checklists.** Huba and Freed (2000) reiterate the importance of using and creating rubrics and checklists, which help to clarify the expectations for writing assignments. Rubrics and checklists also enable students to become self-directed in mastering the content learning.

Introduction:
How to Use This Book

The focus of this research-based book is to demonstrate how to incorporate more writing in the social studies class. Increasing the use of writing is a key way to promote stronger literacy in the content areas. Research shows that using writing in social studies is the best way to help students understand the complex concepts and terms introduced in the content areas. This book provides social studies teachers with the information needed to implement writing activities and assignments that correlate with social studies objectives and goals. The strong research connection in this book helps tie what teachers actually do in the classroom with the most current research available.

Part 1: Writing to Learn in Social Studies

This section is composed of strategies for using writing to learn in social studies. These include vocabulary development, previewing and reviewing, journal-writing, note-taking, and diagramming and mapping. These strategies use writing as a tool for students to process and personalize what they learn so that they are able to synthesize and break down the complex social studies terms and concepts.

Part 2: Writing to Apply in Social Studies

This section offers strategies for using writing to apply new knowledge in social studies: authoring skills, summarizing, and writing applications in all genres. These strategies provide opportunities to utilize the entire writing process to compose a piece of writing that incorporates their social studies knowledge. Teachers may wish to use strategies from Part 1 as building blocks for working toward these application assignments.

Part 3: Assessment

This section describes several holistic assessment options for writing in the social studies classroom. Each strategy listed in the book includes the purpose for and benefits of the strategy and its connection to writing and social studies, the grade levels for which it is appropriate, and the McREL standards that it meets. A step-by-step activity description follows, along with variations, if appropriate, and differentiated instruction to accommodate all types of students. These alterations and suggestions are written for English Language Learners, gifted students, and students who are reading and writing below grade level.

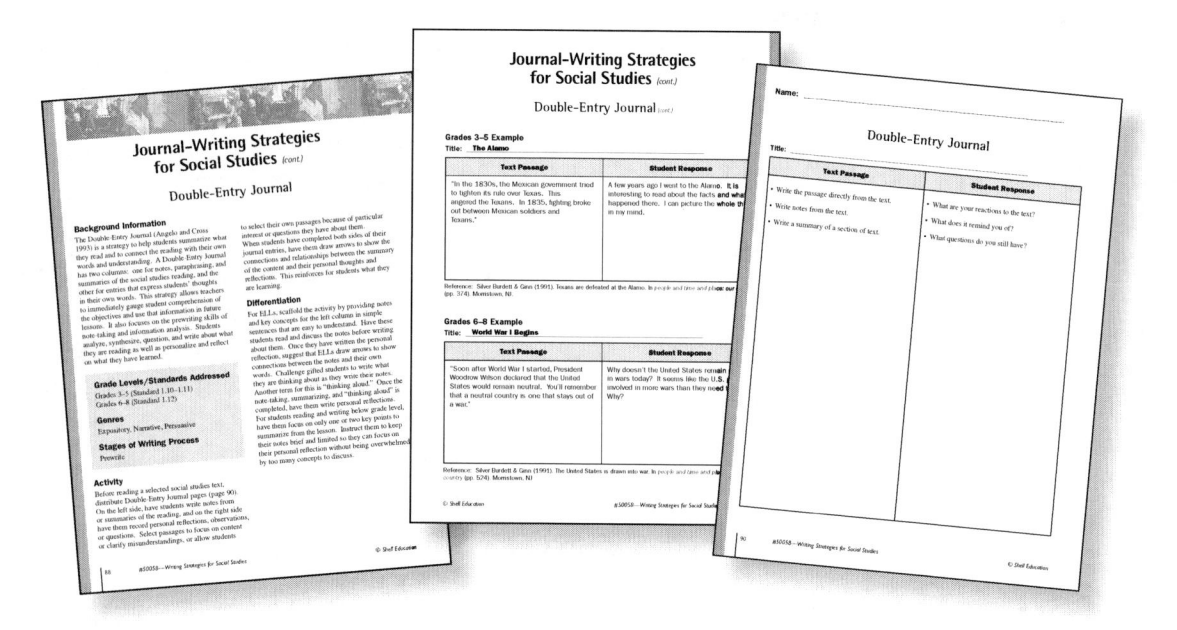

Introduction:
Correlation to McREL Standards

Correlation to Standards

The No Child Left Behind (NCLB) legislation mandates that all states adopt academic standards that identify the skills students will learn in kindergarten through grade 12. While many states had already adopted academic standards prior to NCLB, the legislation set requirements to ensure the standards were detailed and comprehensive.

Standards are designed to focus instruction and guide adoption of curricula. Standards are statements that describe the criteria necessary for students to meet specific academic goals. They define the knowledge, skills, and content students should acquire at each level. Standards are also used to develop standardized tests to evaluate students' academic progress.

In many states today, teachers are required to demonstrate how their lessons meet state standards. State standards are used in the development of Shell Education products, so educators can be assured that they meet the academic requirements of each state.

How to Find Your State Correlations

Shell Education is committed to producing educational materials that are research and standards based. In this effort, all products are correlated to the academic standards of the 50 states, the District of Columbia, and the Department of Defense Dependent Schools. A correlation report customized for your state can be printed directly from the following website: **http://www.shelleducation.com.** If you require assistance in printing correlation reports, please contact Customer Service at 1-800-877-3450.

McREL Compendium

Shell Education uses the Mid-continent Research for Education and Learning (McREL) Compendium to create standards correlations. Each year, McREL analyzes state standards and revises the compendium. By following this procedure, they are able to produce a general compilation of national standards.

Each reading comprehension strategy assessed in this book is based on one or more McREL content standards. The chart on the following page shows the McREL standards that correlate to each lesson used in the book. To see a state-specific correlation, visit the Shell Education website at **http://www.shelleducation.com.**

Identifying Learning Objectives and Goals

When teaching a lesson that involves social studies reading, the first step is to identify the learning objectives and goals for the lesson. The teacher should identify the goals of the lesson and discuss them directly with the students. Their understanding of the expectations and purpose of the lesson will help them to better gauge their own learning. Some of these goals may address language arts standards as well as social studies standards. This is the first step in helping students develop the metacognitive skills necessary for self-monitoring. Planning for reading lessons with the goals in mind allows teachers to determine their objectives and address the learning standards required by the school district, state, and nation. By doing so, teachers naturally build into their lessons a means of assessing students' learning.

Introduction:
Correlation to McREL Standards *(cont.)*

Grades	Standard I	Uses the general skills and strategies of the writing process	Page
1–2, 3–5, 6–8	1.1	Uses prewriting strategies to plan written work	32–36, 47–51, 52–55, 56–59, 60–63, 82–84, 109–111, 112–115, 116–118, 119–122, 123–126, 127–129, 130–134, 135–139, 141–142, 143–145, 154–156, 157–158, 159–162
1–2, 3–5, 6–8	1.2	Uses strategies to draft and revise written work	40–42, 47–51, 52–55, 60–63, 85–87, 141–142, 143–145, 157–158, 159–162
1–2, 3–5, 6–8	1.4	Evaluates own and other's writing	71–73, 146–148, 149–152, 187–188, 189–190, 191–192, 193–195, 196–197, 198–199
3–5, 6–8	1.5	Uses strategies (content, style, and structure) to write for different audiences and purposes (to inform, explain, etc.)	64–67, 75–78, 94–97, 172–173
1–2	1.6	Uses writing and other methods to describe familiar persons, places, objects, or experiences	68–70, 79–81, 91–93, 94–97
1–2, 3–5	1.8, 1.6	Uses strategies to write for a variety of purposes	64–67, 75–78, 94–97, 172–173
3–5, 6–8	1.7, 1.6	Writes expository compositions	166–167, 170–171, 178–179, 180–181
1–2	1.7	Writes in a variety of forms or genres	172–173, 174–175, 176–177, 178–179, 180–181, 182–183
3–5, 6–8	1.8, 1.7	Writes narrative accounts	91–93, 182–183
6–8	1.8	Writes compositions about autobiographical incidents	91–93, 182–183
3–5	1.10	Writes expressive compositions	64–67, 68–70, 71–73, 79–81, 88–90, 91–93, 94–97
3–5, 6–8	1.11, 1.12	Writes in response to literature	68–70, 71–73, 88–90, 149–152, 154–156, 157–158, 159–162, 164–165
6–8	1.11	Writes compositions that address problems/solutions	170–171
3–5	1.12	Writes personal letters	174–175, 176–177
6–8	1.13	Writes business letters and letters of request	174–175, 176–177

Introduction:
Correlation to McREL Standards (cont.)

Grades	Standard 2	Uses the stylistic and rhetorical aspects of writing	Page
1–2	2.1	Uses descriptive words to convey basic ideas	21–24, 37–39
3–5, 6–8	2.1	Uses descriptive language that clarifies and enhances ideas	21–24, 37–39

Grades	Standard 4	Gathers and uses information for research purposes	Page
3–5	4.1	Uses a variety of strategies to plan research	82–84
1–2	4.2	Uses a variety of sources to gather information	28–31, 112–115, 119–122, 123–126, 130–134
3–5	4.3	Uses dictionaries to gather information for research topics	43–45
6–8	4.3	Uses a variety of resource materials to gather information for research topics	25–27, 28–31, 43–45, 82–84
6–8	4.5	Organizes information and ideas from multiple sources in systematic ways	43–45, 99–101, 102–104, 105–107, 109–111, 112–115, 119–122, 123–126, 127–129, 130–134, 168–169
6–8	4.6	Writes research papers	184–185
3–5	4.7	Uses strategies to gather and record information for research topics	25–27, 28–31, 43–45, 99–101, 102–104, 105–107, 109–111, 112–115, 116–118, 119–122, 123–126, 127–129, 130–134
3–5	4.8	Uses strategies to compile information into written reports or summaries	168–169, 184–185

Teaching Social Studies Vocabulary Through Writing

Social Studies Vocabulary and Writing

Extensive research shows that the size of a student's vocabulary is directly related to a student's ability to read (Laflamme 1997). The larger the vocabulary, the easier it is for the student to read. The connection between vocabulary and writing is even stronger. One's ability to write is directly tied to one's ability to understand and use vocabulary words. Unlike with reading, students do not have the benefit of using context clues to determine the meaning of words. As writers, they are creating the context clues!

Becker (1977) has determined that the deficiencies a student may have in vocabulary may lead to poor academic achievement. With the pressure to increase the social studies, technology, and mathematical skills of students, there is no room to fail. Enriching the vocabulary of students is a necessity if we want students to continue to build and learn social studies-related terms.

Because students are exposed to a large number of social studies vocabulary words in the social studies classroom, they need opportunities to interact with these words to become familiar with them and build them into their background knowledge. Students will not internalize and remember these words by reading alone. They must learn to know and understand these words well enough to write about them. Their writing and comprehension skills depend upon it. According to Corona, Spangenberger, and Venet (1998), "At any level, written communication is more effective when a depth of vocabulary and command of language is evident" (p. 26). Research about vocabulary demonstrates the need for an emphasis on writing for students to understand new terms. Writing is the way a student can personalize unfamiliar terms and incorporate them into his or her vocabulary.

National social studies standards also emphasize that students need the ability to communicate their understanding of social studies ideas and information (National Research Council 1996). This means that students should be engaged in activities where they discuss and write about social studies terms and concepts, as well as generate questions, predict answers, and evaluate evidence. Building students' vocabulary will assist teachers in accomplishing this task. The following strategies provide teachers with vocabulary exercises and activities to help build students' vocabulary in the subject of social studies.

So how do students increase their vocabulary in order to incorporate it into their writing? Research suggests that we learn the meaning of words by using them in the context of "old" words we already know and understand (Adams 1990). New learning is continually building on old or previous learning. The same is true for old and new vocabulary words. New vocabulary words are learned by building on known words. We use these "old" words to describe and define new vocabulary. Most of learning is acquired through language (Adams 1990). The learning occurs through accessing prior language and connecting it to new language.

Writing Strategies to Teach Vocabulary in Social Studies

Social Studies Word Wall

Background Information

A Social Studies Word Wall is a display of key vocabulary or concept words. It can be created on a bulletin board or on a large piece of paper taped to the wall. Social Studies Word Walls are an effective way to keep track of new words students are learning and an easy reference for them during class to develop oral and written language. Students will be more apt to use the Word Wall if they are involved with the creation and the upkeep of the wall.

Grade Levels/Standards Addressed

Grades 1–2 (Standard 2.1)
Grades 3–5 (Standard 2.1)
Grades 6–8 (Standard 2.1)

Genres

Expository, Summary, Narrative, Persuasive

Stages of Writing Process

Prewrite, Draft, Revise

Activity

Prepare strips of cardstock that are large enough to be read easily from a distance and ask students to neatly print the vocabulary words. Encourage students to include illustrations for each word, if possible. Designate a spot in the classroom for the Social Studies Word Wall, and reserve a specific area for new vocabulary words. Remind students to use this resource as they write about or learn new concepts. There are many activities that can be incorporated with the Social Studies Word Wall. Select from the activities listed or create activities to best meet the needs of your students:

- **Make a List**—Have students classify the Social Studies Word Wall words by part of speech, roots, prefixes, suffixes, etc.
- **Defining Sentence**—Assign each student a word. Students must create a sentence for the assigned word that gives the definition of the word.
- **What's at the End?**—Identify and discuss words with similar endings.
- **See It, Say It, Chant It, Sing It, and Clap It!**—Find as many different ways as possible to read and spell the words on the Word Wall.
- **Be a Mind Reader**—Have a student give clues about a selected word, while class members try to guess the word. Clues can include the beginning or ending letter, rhyme clues, the definition of its roots, prefixes, or suffixes, number of letters in the word, etc.
- **Guess the Covered Word**—Write sentences on the board using the Social Studies Word Wall words and challenge students to guess which word belongs in each sentence.
- **Find it First!**—Call two students up to the Social Studies Word Wall at a time. Call out a word; see which student can find it first and use it in a sentence.
- **Seek and Find**—Challenge students to search newspapers, brochures, letters, business cards, etc., to highlight Social Studies Word Wall words.
- **Crossword Puzzles**—Have students use the words on the Social Studies Word Wall to make crossword puzzles, exchange the crossword puzzles, and solve them.

Writing Strategies to Teach Vocabulary in Social Studies *(cont.)*

Social Studies Word Wall *(cont.)*

Differentiation

For ELLs, the Social Studies Word Wall is particularly helpful because it exposes the students to important vocabulary words and is an easy reference for students during the lesson. Give ELLs a list of the words to keep at their desks and take home for assignments, if necessary. Encourage gifted students to add more challenging words to the Social Studies Word Wall. These students can generate a list of words they have an interest in learning. Give students reading and writing below grade level a copy of the words to place in their notebooks. They may need repeated explanation of the meanings and use of each word.

Writing Strategies to Teach Vocabulary in Social Studies *(cont.)*

Social Studies Word Wall *(cont.)*

Grades 1–2 Example

My Community

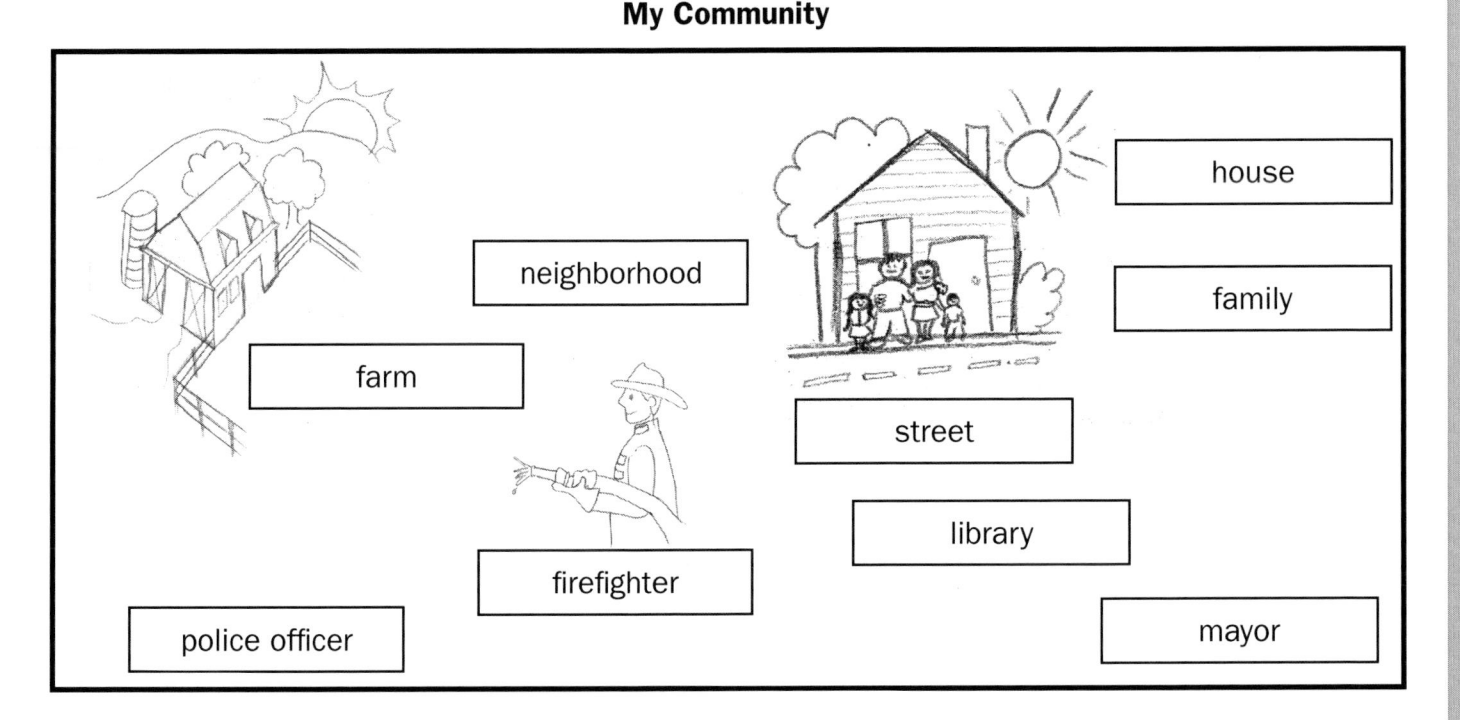

Grades 3–5 Example

The Civil War

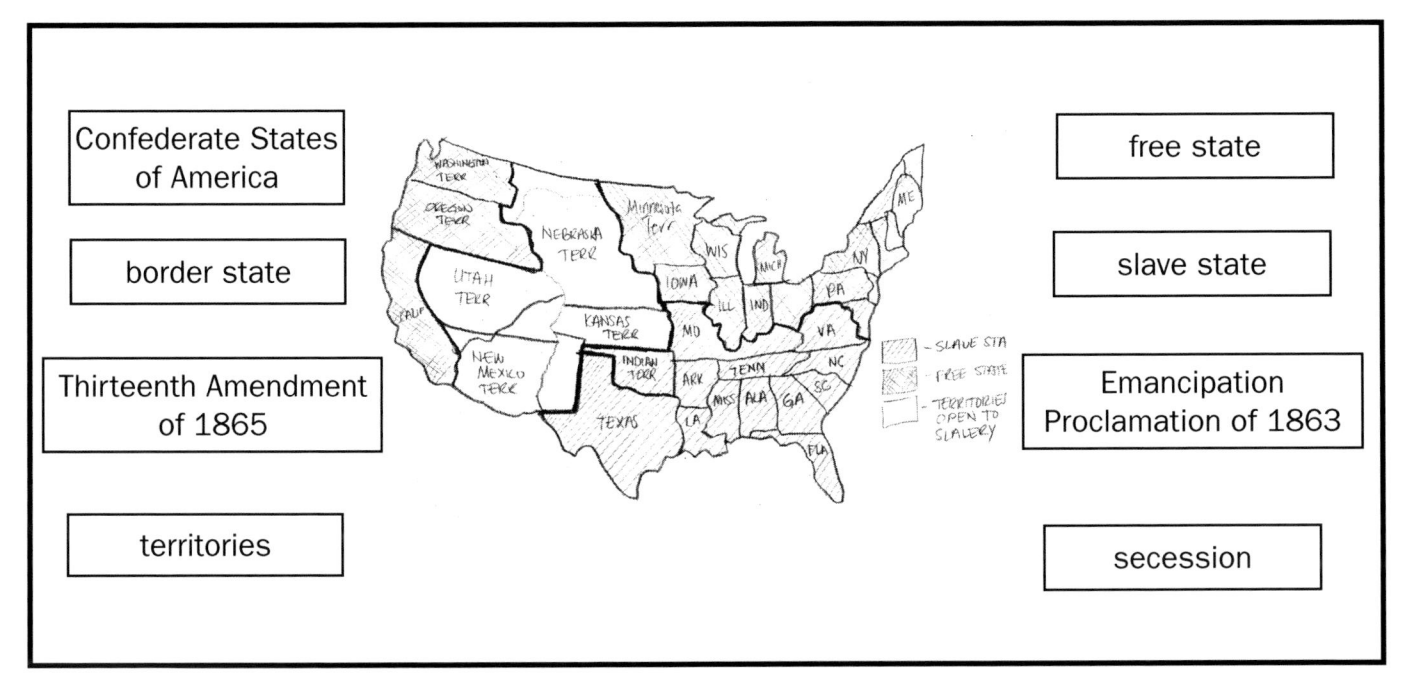

Writing Strategies to Teach Vocabulary in Social Studies (cont.)

Social Studies Word Wall (cont.)

Grades 6–8 Example

Industrial Revolution

child labor	subsidies	urbanization
business expansion	labor issues	
		immigration
tariffs	laissez-faire policies	
		industrialization
banking	labor movement	
land grants	collective bargaining	conservation movement

Writing Strategies to Teach Vocabulary in Social Studies *(cont.)*

Frayer Model

Background Information

The Frayer Model (Frayer, Frederick, and Klausmeier 1969), also known as a word map (Schwartz and Raphael 1985), is a strategy designed to help students understand relationships and similarities between concepts. This strategy uses a graphic organizer to help students understand a concept and recognize similarities and differences between that concept and other concepts being discussed. The framework of the Frayer Model consists of the concept word, the definition, characteristics of the concept word, examples of the concept word, and non-examples of the concept word. A key element of this model is providing an example of what the concept is and what it is not. The Frayer Model is often used when teaching vocabulary, but it can be used to teach and reinforce social studies concepts as well.

Grade Levels/Standards Addressed
Grades 3–5 (Standard 4.7)
Grades 6–8 (Standard 4.3)

Genres
Expository

Stages of Writing Process
Prewrite

Activity

Distribute copies of the Frayer Model graphic organizer (page 27). Have students write the concept of the lesson at the center. This may be a concept phrase or a single word, depending on the needs of the students and the lesson objective. As a class, determine the definition of this concept. Students can use their textbooks or a variety of resources to develop a definition that is clear, concise, and easy to understand. Next, help students determine the characteristics or attributes of this concept. Finally, determine as a class what the concept is and what it is not. Encourage students to generate their own examples and non-examples and allow time for students to discuss their findings with the class. Once students are comfortable using this strategy, they can work in small groups, in pairs, or independently to research different concepts relating to social studies. When the graphic organizer has been completed, students then write a paragraph about this concept using the Frayer Model graphic organizer as a guide.

Differentiation

Place ELLs in groups or pair them with partners to complete the Frayer Model. Working with a partner will help them learn how to complete the Frayer Model, and they will also benefit greatly from the discussions. Call on gifted students to model how to complete the organizer for the class. Gifted students can work with two or three classmates to show the class how to complete the Frayer Model process. The class can learn from watching this discussion, and it encourages gifted students to think through their reasoning. Provide one-on-one instruction during the small group work for students reading and writing below grade level and select an appropriate concept word.

Writing Strategies to Teach Vocabulary in Social Studies (cont.)

Frayer Model (cont.)

Grades 3–5 Example

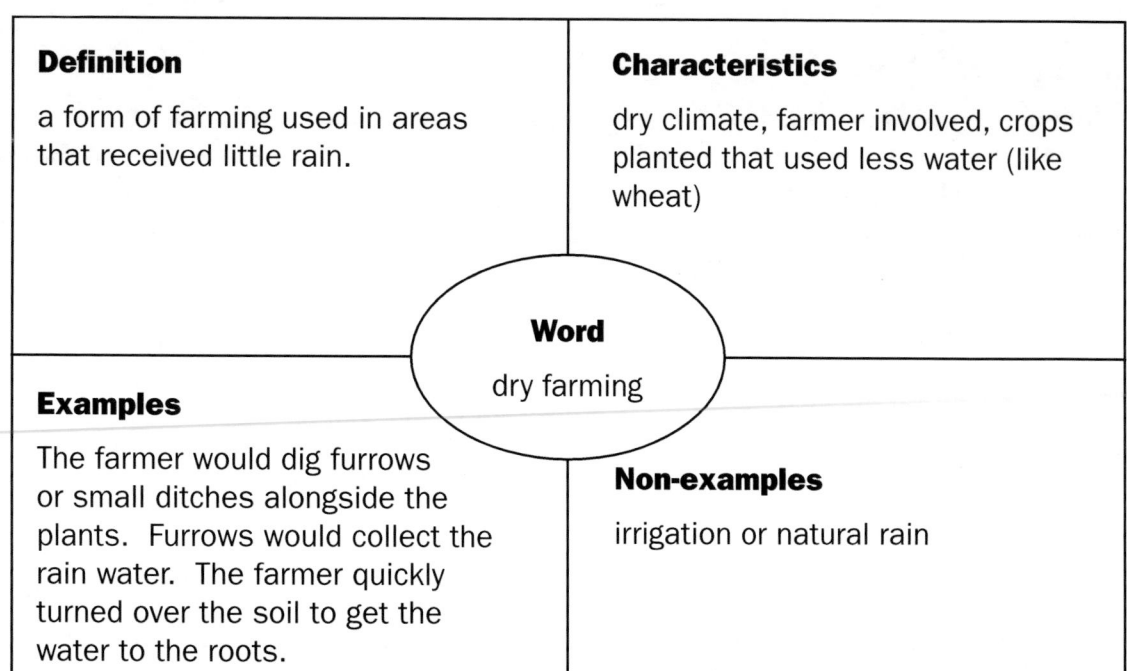

Definition	Characteristics
a form of farming used in areas that received little rain.	dry climate, farmer involved, crops planted that used less water (like wheat)

Word
dry farming

Examples	Non-examples
The farmer would dig furrows or small ditches alongside the plants. Furrows would collect the rain water. The farmer quickly turned over the soil to get the water to the roots.	irrigation or natural rain

Grades 6–8 Example

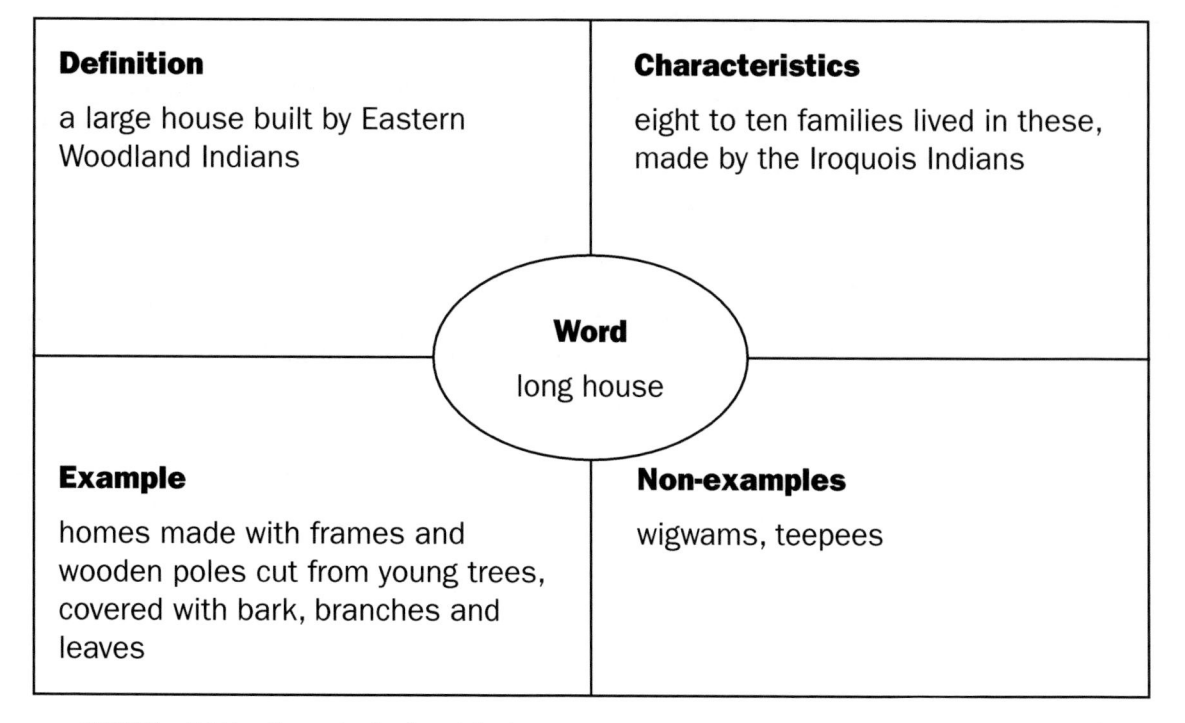

Definition	Characteristics
a large house built by Eastern Woodland Indians	eight to ten families lived in these, made by the Iroquois Indians

Word
long house

Example	Non-examples
homes made with frames and wooden poles cut from young trees, covered with bark, branches and leaves	wigwams, teepees

Name: _____

Frayer Model

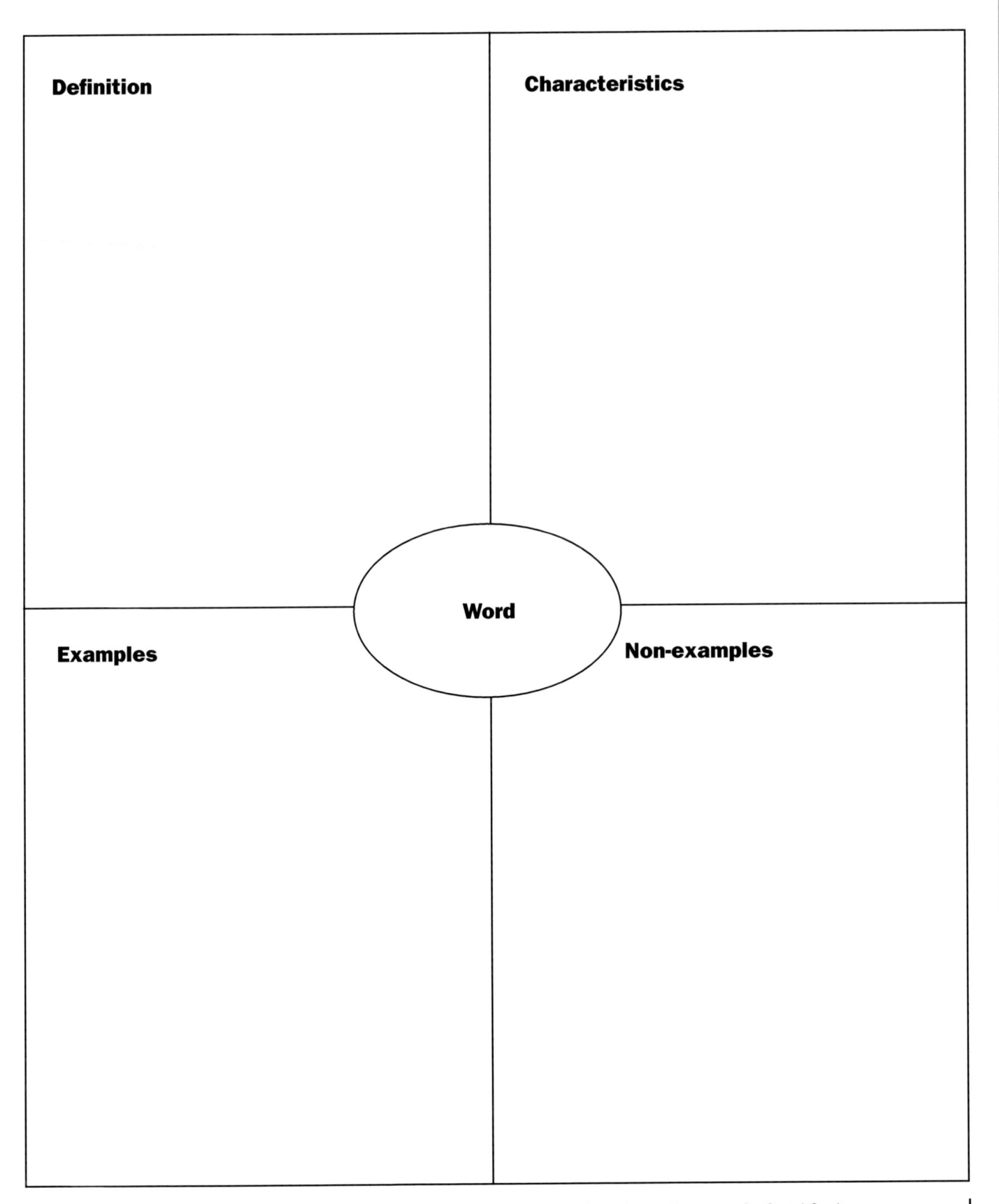

Definition	Characteristics

Word

Examples	Non-examples

Writing Strategies to Teach Vocabulary in Social Studies (cont.)

Concept of Definition Map

Background Information

Using the Concept of Definition Map graphic organizer (Schwartz and Raphael 1985) helps teach definitions of vocabulary words used in social studies. There are many different ways to learn the definition of a term other than simply looking up the dictionary definition. The Concept of Definition Map outlines a variety of ways for students to learn the meaning of a word. It helps them make connections with words when they can look at them in a variety of settings. The Concept of Definition Map makes use of students' senses and their prior knowledge to help them learn new word meanings. The characteristics of the new term are analyzed including the simple definition (What is it?), comparative descriptions (What is it like?), and examples of the new term (What are some examples and illustrations?). These strategies promote long-term memory because students have had an opportunity to personally connect with the word.

Grade Levels/Standards Addressed

Grades 1–2 (Standard 4.2)
Grades 3–5 (Standard 4.7)
Grades 6–8 (Standard 4.3)

Genres

Expository

Stages of Writing Process

Prewrite

Activity

Prior to assigning a reading selection, determine the words that students will not understand or that will be new to them. Select one of these words and write it on the board. Make an overhead transparency of the Concept of Definition Map (page 31) and write the word at the center of the map. Work as a class to complete the map. Students should be encouraged to use all their senses to understand the new word. Ask the following questions:

- What is it?
- What are some things you know about it?
- What is it like?
- What are some examples of it?

Assign students a passage of social studies text that incorporates the new word. Encourage them to add any new information to their maps. Allow time for students to share their maps. Write examples on the board of good definitions and analogies that students have generated.

Differentiation

Pair ELLs with partners to assist them in completing the map. These students will also need reinforcement from the teacher to ensure that they understand the definition(s). Challenge gifted students to complete more than one map using a variety of words. Ask these students to do further research on these words and use a variety of sources other than the textbook. Require older students to cite references used. Students who read and write below grade level can complete a map that includes some of the answers already filled in.

Writing Strategies to Teach Vocabulary in Social Studies *(cont.)*

Concept of Definition Map *(cont.)*

Grades 1–2 Example

Directions: Fill out the different categories for the selected word. Use a dictionary or a thesaurus if necessary.

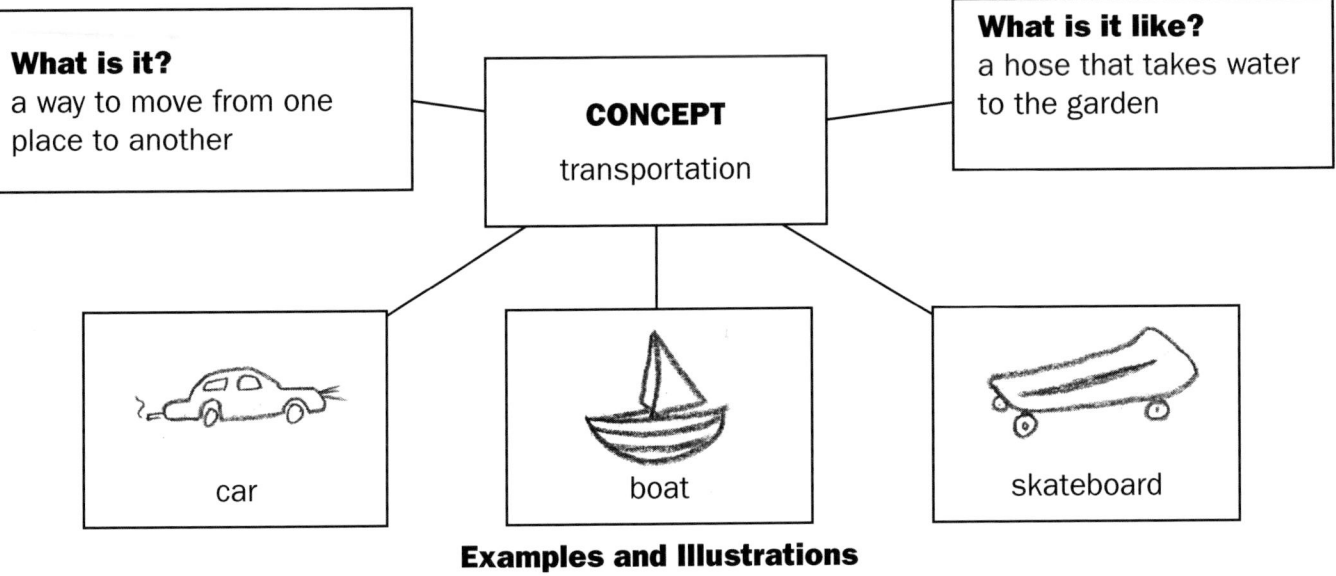

Examples and Illustrations

Grades 3–5 Example

Directions: Fill out the different categories for the selected word. Use a dictionary or a thesaurus if necessary.

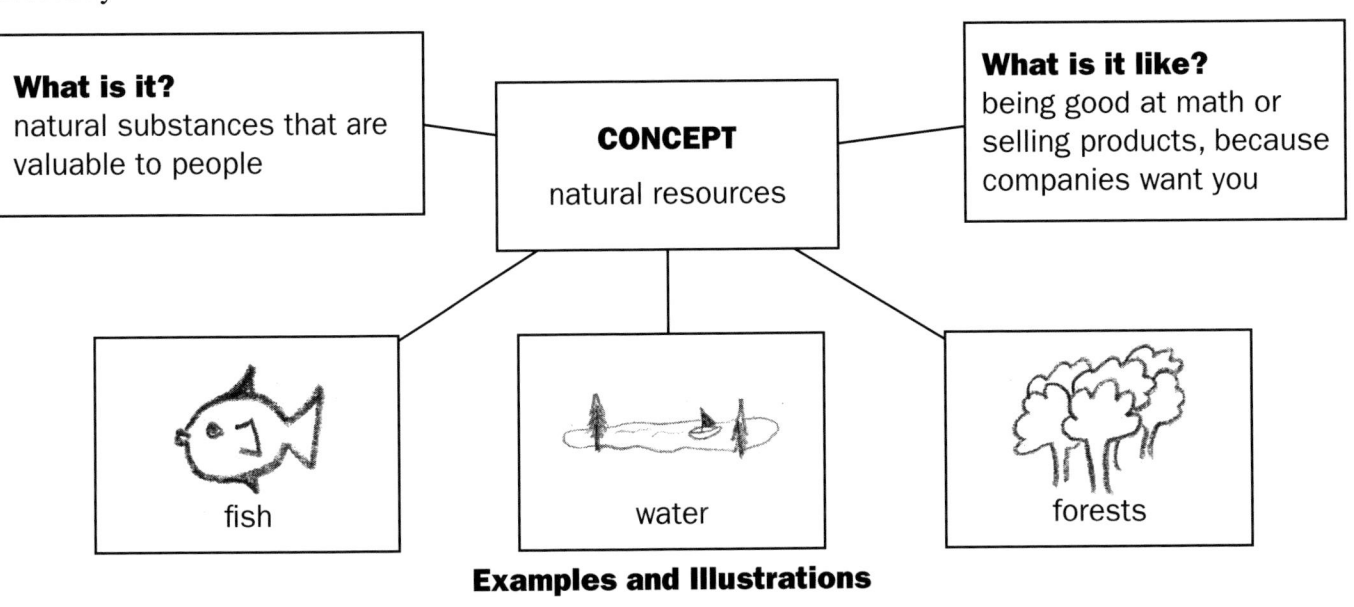

Examples and Illustrations

Writing Strategies to Teach Vocabulary in Social Studies *(cont.)*

Concept of Definition Map *(cont.)*

Grades 6–8 Example

Directions: Fill out the different categories for the selected word. Use a dictionary or a thesaurus if necessary.

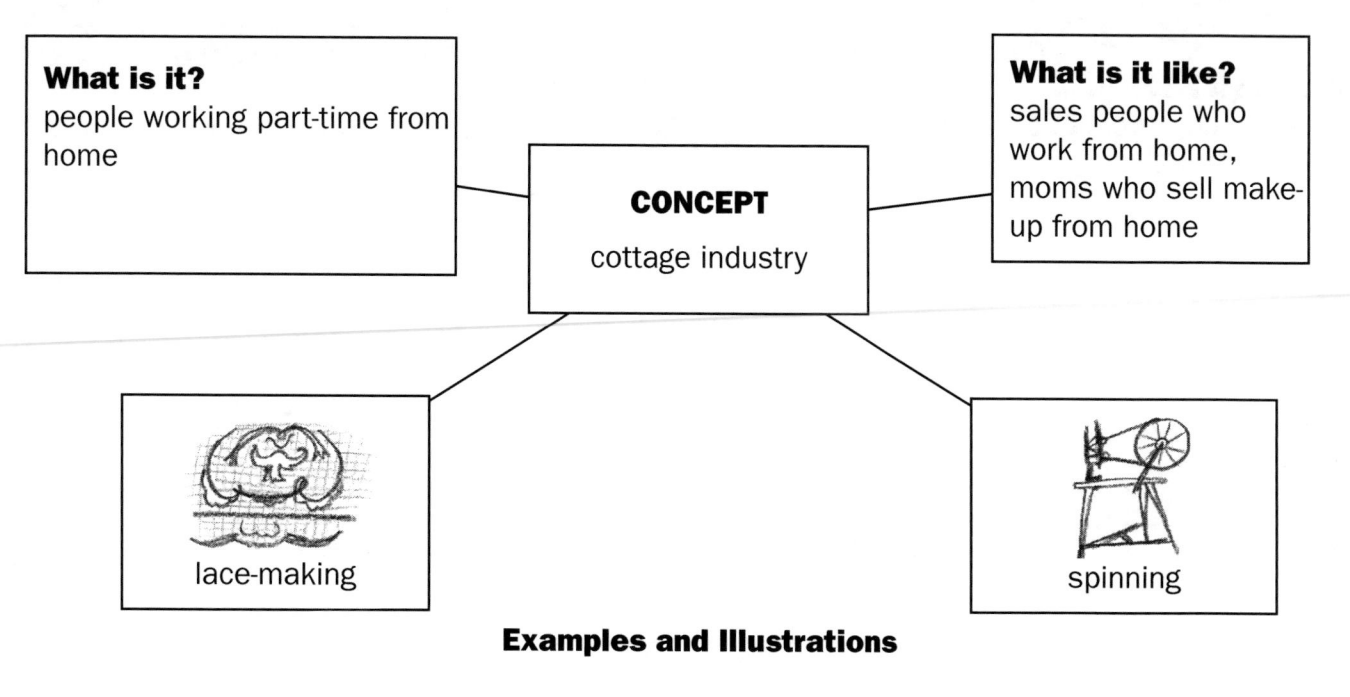

What is it?
people working part-time from home

CONCEPT
cottage industry

What is it like?
sales people who work from home, moms who sell make-up from home

lace-making

spinning

Examples and Illustrations

Name: _____

Concept of Definition Map

Directions: Fill out the different categories for the selected word. Use a dictionary or a thesaurus if necessary.

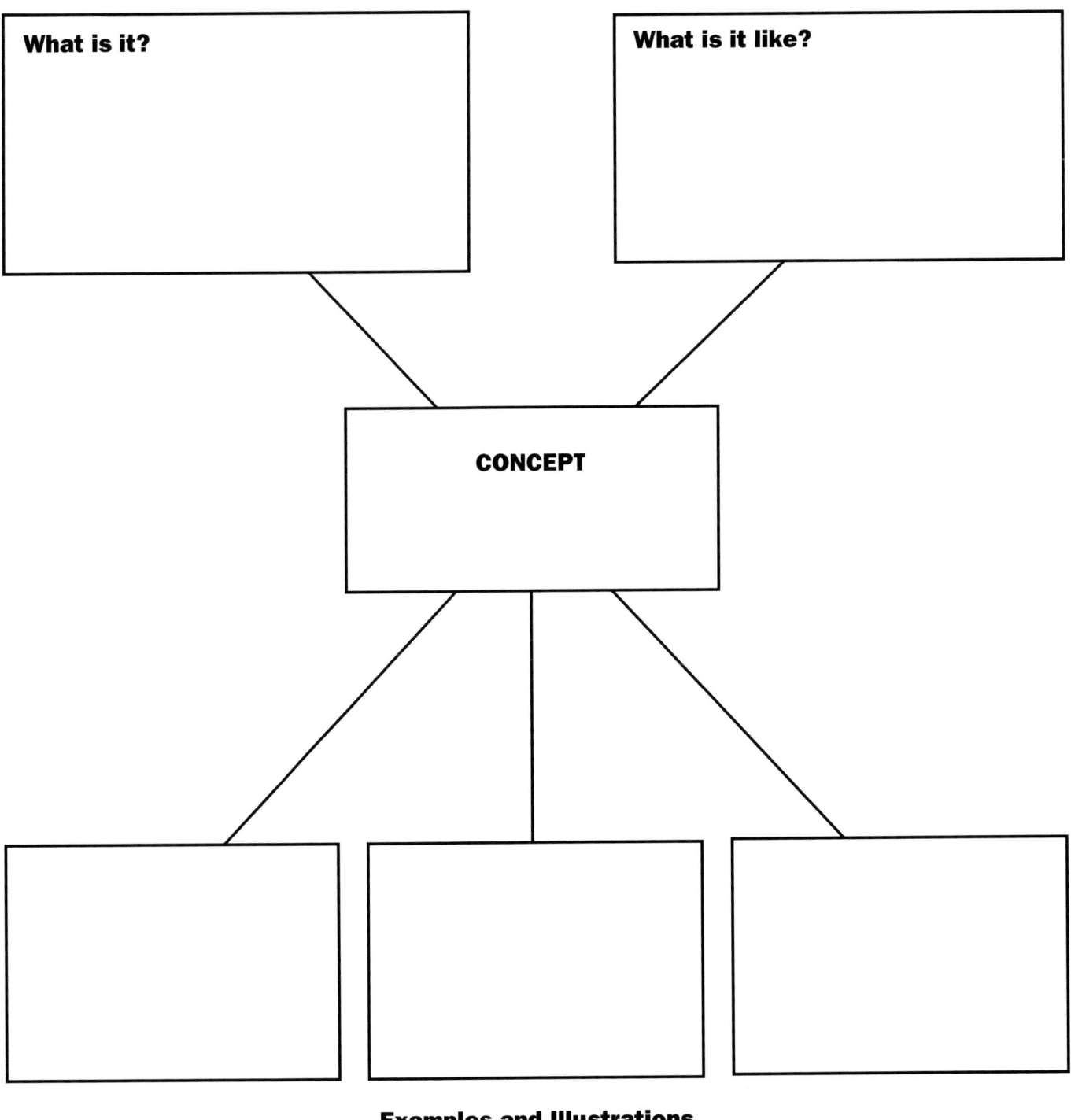

What is it?

What is it like?

CONCEPT

Examples and Illustrations

Writing Strategies to Teach Vocabulary in Social Studies *(cont.)*

List-Group-Label

Background Information

The List-Group-Label (Taba 1967) classification strategy encourages brainstorming to categorize and organize social studies vocabulary in relation to the text. Students combine their prior knowledge about concepts with instruction from the teacher, and then organize the information into categories. This activity can be done at the beginning of a lesson to introduce students to new words and concepts or following a lesson as a review of concepts. Most words are associated with other words and grouping these words in meaningful ways clarifies understanding of words and their meanings. Students can also see hierarchical relationships between words, as well as word parts and word associations. This activity is the bridge between students' background knowledge and the new social studies vocabulary being introduced.

Grade Levels/Standards Addressed

Grades 1–2 (Standard 1.1)
Grades 3–5 (Standard 1.1)
Grades 6–8 (Standard 1.1)

Genres

Expository

Stages of Writing Process

Prewrite

Activity

Prior to the lesson, select a word or phrase that describes the topic of the lesson. Write this word or phrase on the center of the board or of a transparency. Ask students to think of words that are associated with this word and list them on the board. As students suggest words, encourage them to explain the connection to the focus word. This will help eliminate words that are unrelated to the focus word. Allow students to receive assistance from other students to justify their words.

After students have generated a list of 20–30 words, distribute copies or transparencies of the List-Group-Label activity sheet (page 36) to individual students, partners, or small groups. Ask students to group the words into categories based on attributes, characteristics, or features that the words have in common and assign each category a label. Students may need to generate further categories to group all of the words. Some words may need to be eliminated if they do not fit into the categories. Students should continue explaining and justifying their decisions for the selected categories and labels and placement of words in the categories. Remind them to add any additional vocabulary words to the categories if possible.

Writing Strategies to Teach Vocabulary in Social Studies *(cont.)*

List-Group-Label *(cont.)*

Activity *(cont.)*

After categorizing and grouping the words, meet back together as a class. Invite each group to share its version of categorizing and organizing the vocabulary words. Engage the class in a discussion until an agreement can be reached on the categories, labels, and the respective words included in each category. Again, students can continue to add words to the map as they think of them. Students may need to reorganize or re-label categories and relocate words before they reach a consensus. Students must continue justifying the categories they have selected by presenting a rationale.

Keep the students focused on words and categories that are directly related to the lesson objectives. The more the students describe and explain their rationales for the categories and words selected, the more they will make associations to new words.

Variations

Present the class with a list of words (rather than have the students generate the words) and ask the students to individually, or in small groups, determine how to classify the words and select the labels for those categories. Or, conduct the brainstorming session, then scaffold the remainder of the lesson by providing the group labels.

Differentiation

Provide ELLs with resource books or pictures during the brainstorming process so that they can locate words. Use several words to explain each word associated with the topic so that ELLs can better understand. Take extra care to make sure all of the words and phrases on the board are clearly defined and understood by the students reading and writing below grade level. Both ELLs and students reading and writing below grade level will benefit from working in mixed-ability groups. Encourage gifted students to work on generating a list independently or to reclassify the words into alternate categories.

Writing Strategies to Teach Vocabulary in Social Studies (cont.)

List-Group-Label (cont.)

Grades 1–2 Example

Topic: __Transportation__

List

Airplanes	helicopters	horse and buggy	trucks	ships
wagons	train	cars	horseback	paddle boats

Categories

Water Transportation	**Need Animals**	**Wheels**	**Can Fly**
ships	horse and buggy	cars, trucks	airplanes
paddle boats	horseback	trains	helicopters
	wagons	wagons	

Grades 3–5 Example

Topic: __Famous Faces__

List

Harriet Tubman	Elizabeth Cady Stanton	Martin Luther King Jr.
Harry Truman	Jackie Robinson	Susan B. Anthony
Clara Barton	Thomas Jefferson	Franklin D. Roosevelt

Categories

African Americans	**Presidents**	**Women**
Jackie Robinson	Harry Truman	Harriet Tubman
Harriet Tubman	Franklin D. Roosevelt	Clara Barton
Martin Luther King, Jr.	Thomas Jefferson	Elizabeth Cady Stanton
		Susan B. Anthony

Writing Strategies to Teach Vocabulary in Social Studies *(cont.)*

List-Group-Label *(cont.)*

Grades 6–8 Example

Topic: **Places of World War II**

List

Okinawa	Pearl Harbor	Romania	Yugoslavia
Germany	Finland	Bulgaria	France
Iwo Jima	Sweden	Libya	Luxemburg
Spain	Switzerland	Italy	Belgium
Midway Island	Austria	USSR	Great Britain
Ireland	Hungary	Poland	

Categories

Axis Powers	Neutral Countries	East Asia and Pacific	Allies
Finland	Spain	Okinawa	Great Britain
Germany	Turkey	Iwo Jima	France
Austria	Saudi Arabia	Pearl Harbor	Luxemburg
Hungary	Ireland	Midway Island	Poland
Romania	Sweden		USSR
Italy	Switzerland		Yugoslavia
Bulgaria			Belgium
Libya			

List-Group-Label

Directions: Write in the topic, then make a list of words about the topic. Look at the list and create categories of related words. Be sure to label each category.

Topic: _____

List

_____   _____   _____

_____   _____   _____

_____   _____   _____

_____   _____   _____

_____   _____   _____

_____   _____   _____

_____   _____   _____

Categories

_____   _____   _____

_____   _____   _____

_____   _____   _____

_____   _____   _____

_____   _____   _____

_____   _____   _____

Writing Strategies to Teach Vocabulary in Social Studies (cont.)

Vocabulary Self-Collection

Background Information

Haggard (1986a, 1986b) designed the Vocabulary Self-Collection strategy to help students create a list of vocabulary words they would be interested in learning and researching. The strategy is meant to stimulate vocabulary growth. Research shows that the more exposure students have to the written word, the more their vocabulary increases. By generating lists of words to study, students become more sensitive to and aware of words and their meanings.

Grade Levels/Standards Addressed

Grades 1–2 (Standard 2.1)
Grades 3–5 (Standard 2.1)
Grades 6–8 (Standard 2.1)

Genres

Expository

Stages of Writing Process

Prewrite

Activity

Instruct students to create a list of words from their social studies reading materials that they are interested in studying. The words should be of interest to them. Have students review their lists and nominate one of the words to be studied by the class. As you write these words on the board or on an overhead transparency, ask students to define them and justify the selection of each word.

Clarify the meaning of each word and clear up any misunderstandings, consulting a dictionary if needed. Students may ask each other questions about the words and their definitions. After the discussion, challenge the class to decide which words should make the final cut. For example, delete words that most students already know, duplicates of words, and words of little interest to the students. Have students write down the selected words and their meanings in their Vocabulary Journal (see pages 75–78) and post them on the Social Studies Word Wall (see pages 21–24). Incorporate these words into lessons and writing activities that will reinforce definitions and understanding. Encourage students to use these words as often as possible in their own writing to move the new vocabulary words into their expressive languages.

Differentiation

During the discussion, clarify and elaborate further on some definitions if necessary to ensure that ELLs understand the meanings. Use visuals as well as thorough descriptions. Challenge gifted students to document the use of the vocabulary words in their personal writing assignments. Students who read and write below grade level may need assistance articulating the meanings of difficult words, so encourage them to use visuals or drawings, if needed.

Writing Strategies to Teach Vocabulary in Social Studies *(cont.)*

Vocabulary Self-Collection *(cont.)*

Grades 1–2 Example

Text:	As farm prices fell lower and lower, more and more farmers could not pay off their loans.
Nominated Words:	farmer, lower, pay, loans, farm

Grades 3–5 Example

Text:	Times were especially hard for minority groups such as African Americans, Mexican Americans, and American Indians. Members of these groups were usually the last people hired and the first people fired. It was a very difficult time.
Nominated Words:	minority, groups, fired, African Americans, Mexican Americans, American Indians

Writing Strategies to Teach Vocabulary in Social Studies *(cont.)*

Vocabulary Self-Collection *(cont.)*

Grades 6–8 Example

Text:	Franklin Delano Roosevelt was elected into office and he began creating government programs to help people work. Many of these programs were known as the New Deal. The New Deal created many opportunities for people that had nothing.
Nominated Words:	creating, elected, programs, New Deal, opportunities

Writing Strategies to Teach Vocabulary in Social Studies *(cont.)*

Possible Sentences

Background Information

Moore and Moore (1986) designed the Possible Sentences strategy as a way to teach vocabulary words introduced in a text. Other benefits of this strategy include making predictions about reading, providing a purpose for reading, and encouraging interest in text. Students learn to make predictions about new words, check their predictions, and use the text to rewrite and refine their predictions.

Grade Levels/Standards Addressed

Grades 1–2 (Standard 1.2)
Grades 3–5 (Standard 1.2)
Grades 6–8 (Standard 1.2)

Genres

Expository

Stage of Writing Process

Draft, Revise

Activity

Make a list of important vocabulary words from the social studies text and write them on the board or a transparency. Read each word aloud to model correct pronunciation. Instruct students to select two words from the list to use in one sentence that might appear in a social studies text. Record sentences on the board and underline each vocabulary word. Encourage students to generate sentences until all the vocabulary words have been used in at least one sentence. Remind students that good writers edit and revise their work, and have them read through the sentences again to make any needed changes.

Next ask students to read the selected text and compare the class sentences with the actual sentences in the text. Students should take notes (or draw pictures for younger students) on meanings of words. After reading the text, carefully examine the sentences to see if they are written accurately. Have students explain how to edit and revise sentences as needed. Call on students to write revised sentences independently using their new knowledge and understanding of these vocabulary words.

Differentiation

Preview the meanings of the vocabulary words with ELLs to ensure understanding. Encourage ELLs to draw pictures or write short phrases if they are not yet ready to write sentences. Encourage gifted students to write multiple sentences using various forms of the words and more complicated sentence structures. Scaffold the strategy for students who read and write below grade level by providing sentence frames. Also, encourage these students to extend their sentences by adding additional information.

Writing Strategies to Teach Vocabulary in Social Studies (cont.)

Possible Sentences (cont.)

Grades 1–2 Example

Vocabulary Words:

buyers, sellers, goods, services

Possible Sentences/Before Reading:

<u>Buyers</u> buy things.
<u>Sellers</u> sell things.
<u>Goods</u> are things that people like.
<u>Services</u> are things you serve.

Revised Sentences/After Reading:

<u>Buyers</u> buy things that they need.
<u>Sellers</u> sell to their customers.
<u>Goods</u> are things that sellers make to sell to their customers.
<u>Services</u> are things that people can do to make money.

Grades 3–5 Example

Vocabulary Words:

ocean, mountains, bay, rivers

Possible Sentences/Before Reading:

We live near the <u>Pacific Ocean</u>.
The <u>mountains</u> are high.
We go to the <u>bay</u> to swim and play in the water.
The <u>rivers</u> go under the freeway.

Revised Sentences/After Reading:

The <u>rivers</u> begin high in the <u>mountains</u> and flow down into the <u>ocean.</u>
The <u>bay</u> is important to our community because the ships can dock there to bring in things from other places.

Writing Strategies to Teach Vocabulary in Social Studies *(cont.)*

Possible Sentences *(cont.)*

Grades 6–8 Example

Vocabulary Words:

suffrage movement, Elizabeth Cady Stanton, Susan B. Anthony, Declaration of Sentiments, National Woman Suffrage Association

Possible Sentences/Before Reading:

<u>Elizabeth Cady Stanton</u> and <u>Susan B. Anthony</u> were important to the woman <u>suffrage movement</u>.
<u>Elizabeth Cady Stanton</u> wrote the <u>Declaration of Sentiments</u>.
<u>Susan B. Anthony</u> founded the <u>National Woman Suffrage Association</u>.

Revised Sentences/After Reading:

<u>Elizabeth Cady Stanton</u> and <u>Susan B. Anthony</u> were two key leaders in the woman <u>suffrage movement</u> of the mid-1800s.
<u>Elizabeth Cady Stanton</u> wrote the <u>Declaration of Sentiments</u>, which was approved at the women's rights convention in Seneca Falls, New York.
<u>Susan B. Anthony</u> and <u>Stanton</u>, who served as president, founded the <u>National Woman Suffrage Association</u>.

Writing Strategies to Teach Vocabulary in Social Studies *(cont.)*

Word Trails

Background Information

A strong relationship exists between word knowledge and reading comprehension. Without word knowledge, readers read less and are more apt to be poor readers (Anderson and Freebody 1985). Seldom do words stand alone, isolated from and unrelated to other words. The Word Trails strategy helps students build connections or "trails" from unknown words to familiar ones. Students need to have a repertoire of strategies to use when they face unknown words in their reading. The Word Trails strategy offers a way to build those bridges.

Grade Levels/Standards Addressed

Grades 3–5 (Standard 4.3, 4.7)
Grades 6–8 (Standard 4.3, 4.5)

Genres

Expository

Stages of Writing Process

Prewrite

Activity

Introduce a new word and then build "trails" and connections from other words to the new word. There are five main trails that connect words:

- **root words**—Many social studies words have similar root words. Knowing these can help students determine meaning.

- **prefixes and suffixes**—Recognizing and identifying prefixes or suffixes in a word can help determine its meaning.

- **synonyms or similar words**—Words become "friends" and can help students remember definitions. What are other words that have the same or similar meaning to the new word? What are examples of this word?

- **antonyms**—Identifying opposites is an effective way to clarify word meaning. What are the words that mean the opposite of this new word? What are non-examples of the word?

Distribute copies of the Word Trails map (page 45) and have students identify the trails from this word to other words. When finished, discuss the findings of the students. Primary grade teachers may want to complete the Word Trails map as a class, then post it on the Word Wall (pages 21–24). Students can add these words and their trails to their Vocabulary Journals (pages 75–78).

Differentiation

Preteach ELLs how to use the Word Trails map, so they understand the format. Consider also preteaching the roots, prefixes, and suffixes that will be addressed during the whole-class lesson so these students will be able to recognize them and apply meaning to the unknown vocabulary word. Use visuals whenever possible. Encourage gifted students to study additional or related vocabulary words and present and explain their Word Trails maps to the class. Limit the number of vocabulary words for students reading and writing below grade level to allow them to focus on a few words.

Writing Strategies to Teach Vocabulary in Social Studies *(cont.)*

Word Trails *(cont.)*

Grades 3–5 Example

Part of Speech		Synonyms or Similar Words
verb		break away, separate

secede

pull out, become independent, split up

Antonyms		Root Words, Prefixes, and Suffixes
come together, unite		secedere (Latin) = to withdraw

Grades 6–8 Example

Part of Speech		Synonyms or Similar Words
verb		answer, reply, respond

interrogate

to examine, to question

Antonyms		Root Words, Prefixes, and Suffixes
answer, reply, repond		interrogatus (Latin) = to question

Name: _____

Word Trails

Directions: Write the word that you are studying in the center box. Use resources to determine the root words, prefixes and suffixes, synonyms or similar words, and antonyms, and write them in the Word Trails graphic organizer.

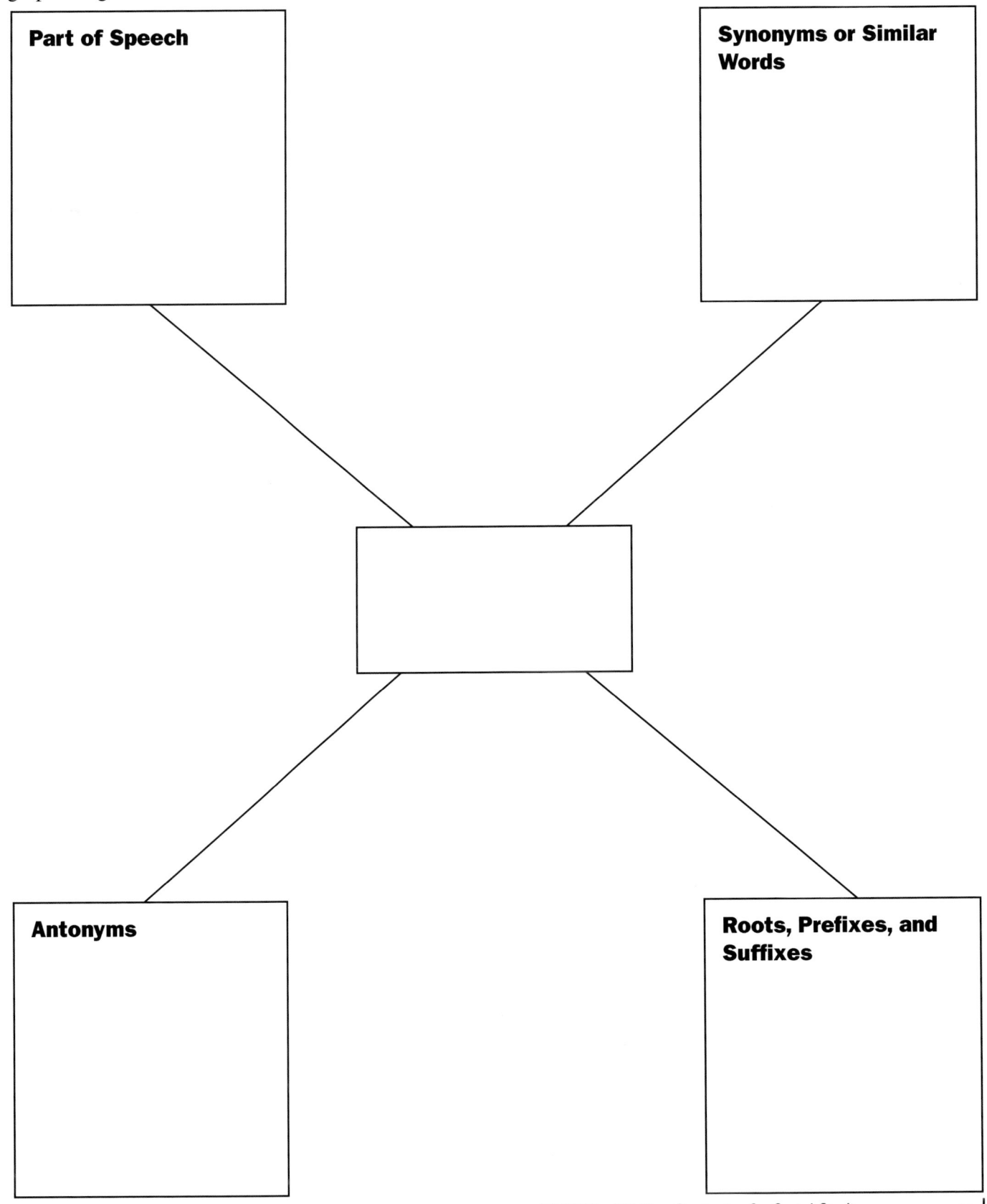

Part of Speech

Synonyms or Similar Words

Antonyms

Roots, Prefixes, and Suffixes

Using Writing to Preview and Review in Social Studies

Activating Prior Knowledge in Social Studies

Research shows that activating background knowledge increases the comprehension that students have (Christen and Murphy 1991). Accessing the students' prior knowledge opens the doors for the new knowledge to find a place. Teachers who link new information to students' background knowledge encourage curiosity and provide a purpose for the new information. This enables the teacher to build on this knowledge. Students are able to make personal connections and incorporate these new thoughts and ideas into what they read and write about.

Prior knowledge can be defined as any information that we know on a given topic before we begin learning new information.

Reviewing and Spiral Knowledge

We all use scripts and categorical rules to interpret the world. When new information arises, our brains work to see how it fits with our predetermined ideas and scripts (Widmayer et al 2004). Throughout our lives we add to our knowledge base and it continues to grow. This is known as spiral knowledge (Poplin 1988, as cited by Dechant 1991).

Using Expressive Writing

Expressive writing leads to the discovery of and the reinforcement of concepts being taught, so it is appropriate for reviewing in social studies. Fulwiler (1980) states, "Every time students write, they individualize instruction; the act of silent writing, even for five minutes, generates ideas, observations, emotions…regular writing makes it harder for students to remain passive" (page 69). In the social studies classroom, expressive writing enables students to turn quantitative information into qualitative information. Students put the information in their own words and begin to own it. Writing is another way for the brain to make sense of information and learning (Emig 1977).

When students use writing as a strategy to help them make sense of what they are reading and learning, they are writing to learn. This is often called expressive writing *in the content areas*. It is a vital piece of the content area curriculum because it allows students the opportunity to express their ideas about and respond to what they are learning.

There is a variety of expressive writing activities: journals, KWL (Ogle 1986), T-List, free writes, dialogue journals (Atwell 1984; Harste, Short, and Burke 1988), problem analyses, learning logs, peer dialogues, and many more. Many of these strategies will be explained and described in this section of the book. With expressive writing, students are encouraged to use their own vocabulary, and the emphasis is on the content and understanding of the student, not on the writing mechanics. Hamilton-Weiler (1988) explains that this kind of writing is ". . . a way into or means of learning, a way into understanding through articulating."

Writing Strategies for Previewing and Reviewing in Social Studies

KWL Chart

Background Information

The KWL Chart (Know-Want to Know-Learn), introduced by Donna Ogle in 1986, is a way to activate student knowledge and encourage active thinking in social studies. This interactive study approach also shows students how reading, writing, research, and observation further develop their knowledge of a particular subject.

The KWL Chart is used prior to a social studies unit or lesson to engage students in writing about what they already know about the topic. Students also write any questions they have about the topic. After the reading, experiment, or observation, students write what they learned. They also review their information in the first column to see if it needs to be revised and check to see if all their questions were answered from the lesson. In this way, students engage in the prewriting process of gathering information and use the skill of editing and revising information, when necessary.

Grade Levels/Standards Addressed

Grades 1–2 (Standard 1.1)
Grades 3–5 (Standard 1.1)
Grades 6–8 (Standard 1.1)

Genres

Expository

Stages of Writing Process

Prewrite

Activity

Distribute copies of the KWL Chart (page 51) and have students write the topic at the top. Before reading, researching, or observing, ask students to list in the K column all the information that they know—even if it may not be correct—about the topic. Next have them list in the W column what they want to know about the subject. Encourage them to think of interesting and pertinent questions, just as good researchers do. After reading the text or completing a social studies activity, instruct students to review their charts. First have them look at the K column and see if the information they listed as prior knowledge was correct. Have students delete or rewrite statements so that they are accurate. Students may need to use more description or more words to share accurate information. Next, have students look at the W column to see if all the questions were answered in the text. If not, students may need to find an alternate source to find the answer. After the discussion, have students write in the L column what they learned.

Variation

For primary grade students, recreate the KWL template on a large piece of butcher paper and complete it as a class. Invite students to dictate a sentence or question for you to write on the chart, or allow individual students the opportunity to write on the chart.

Writing Strategies for Previewing and Reviewing in Social Studies *(cont.)*

KWL Chart *(cont.)*

Variation *(cont.)*

The KWL Chart can be extended to include other categories or columns:

- **Categories of Information We Expect to See**—This addition directs students to anticipate the categories of information the author may provide in the reading selection. Students can use this same strategy of matching information with a topic when planning a writing assignment.

- **Still Want to Learn (KWLS)**—This extension encourages students to articulate any other questions they might wish to explore, and these ideas may provide a springboard for independent research or future writing activities.

- **How to Find Out (KWLSH)**—This category requires students to think about how they might investigate their questions and develops research skills. See grades 6–8 example on page 50.

Differentiation

Pair ELLs with partners who can help discuss and articulate thoughts and ideas on the subject before completing the KWL Chart. This will eliminate confusion resulting from the differences in language and the learning of new social studies vocabulary. Consider providing sentence stems to assist these students in formulating their contributions: *I know that, What is, and I wonder.* Encourage gifted students to add new categories and conduct research independently or in groups. If time allows, these students can present their research findings to the class to enhance the lesson topic. Prior to introducing a new unit of study, inform students reading and writing below grade level of the next topic of study. Provide them with additional time to access their prior knowledge on the topic to assist them in the reading task. Have resources available for students to read before completing the KWL chart.

Writing Strategies for Previewing and Reviewing in Social Studies *(cont.)*

KWL Chart *(cont.)*

Grades 1–2 Example (before reading)

Topic: **The Medical Doctor**

K	W	L
I know that a doctor needs to go to school for a long time. Doctors help people get better. Doctors give you medicine.	Who decides who gets to be a doctor? Why do doctors wear those blue clothes? What is that thing that hangs around their necks? How can I be a doctor? Why do some doctors work at hospitals and some work at an office?	

Grades 3–5 Example (after reading)

Topic: **Hawaii Joins the United States**

K	W	L
I know that Hawaii was second to the last state added to the United States. There was a queen named Liliuokalani.	Why did it take that long? How did Hawaii become a state?	Not everyone agreed with the way that Hawaii was added. Queen Liliuokalani was forced by the representatives of the Republic of Hawaii to give up the throne. President McKinley agreed to the annnexation. Both houses of Congress passed the resolution with a two-thirds vote.

Writing Strategies for Previewing and Reviewing in Social Studies (cont.)

KWL Chart (cont.)

Grades 6-8 Example (after reading)

Topic: __Manifest Destiny__

K	W	L	S	H
Manifest Destiny had to do with taking over the western United States before it belonged to the U.S. It caused a lot of conflicts with other groups and countries.	What land became a part of the U.S.? Which wars were a part of it? Where did the name Manifest Destiny come from?	Journalist John L. O'Sullivan coined the term in 1845. Texas declared independence from Mexico, fought the Texas Revolution, and became a U.S. state. The U.S. took over American Indian land, which gave way to "Indian Removal" programs.	How did the public feel about Manifest Destiny? What would the U.S. be like today without the land we took over? Did the U.S. ever try to compensate the American Indians for taking away their lands?	We could do research on the Internet for the first and third question. We would have to talk about the second question as a class. There isn't a real answer to that.

Topic: _____

KWL Chart

K	W	L

Writing Strategies for Previewing and Reviewing in Social Studies (cont.)

Think Sheet

Background Information

The Think Sheet strategy enables students to examine their knowledge on a social studies topic before reading about it, and then compare that to what they learn after reading or discussion. This strategy provides practice in generating information related to a topic, which students need to learn for the prewriting phase. Students also use the revising skill of analyzing existing notes for missing or incorrect information. Both skills are keys to successful writing.

Standards Addressed

Grades 1–2 (Standard 1.1–1.2)
Grades 3–5 (Standard 1.1–1.2)
Grades 6–8 (Standard 1.1–1.2)

Genres

Expository

Stages of Writing Process

Prewrite, Revise

Preparation

Prior to a reading, lecture, or observation, formulate some questions about the topic that will activate prior knowledge, generate thinking, and promote curiosity. Then add the questions to the Think Sheet (page 55).

Activity

Distribute copies of the prepared Think Sheet or recreate it on a transparency or on the board. Present the main issue to the class, and ask students to answer the questions and write down what they know. Be sure to encourage them to write any questions that they have about the topic because

questions are the foundation of scientific research. Collect students' Think Sheets then assign the reading or complete the activity as planned. Redistribute the Think Sheets so that students can use their new knowledge to edit their original answers. Ask questions such as these: *How did your knowledge change after this activity? Can you add any additional information? Do you have any questions that were not answered? Were any of your original thoughts inaccurate?* Encourage students to write additional questions they have on the topic. Allow students to share what they have learned from the reading and encourage them to make connections between their questions, their thoughts, and the information presented in the text.

Variation

Complete this activity as a class with primary grade students. Lead a brief discussion about each question, and ask students to help develop an answer. You may choose specific students to help write some or all of the sentences on the board.

Differentiation

Spend time clarifying the questions that are being asked for ELLs. Remind students that these are new questions and they are not expected to know the answers. Encourage gifted students to conduct further research to answer the questions left unanswered and share their findings with the class. Scaffold the Think Sheet with some completed responses for students reading and writing below grade level. If the reading level is too high for these students, read aloud to them or have them do a paired reading.

Writing Strategies for Previewing and Reviewing in Social Studies *(cont.)*

Think Sheet *(cont.)*

Grades 1–2 Example (before reading)

Main Issue: <u>Family Types</u>

Teacher Questions	My Questions/Thoughts
1. Can you name the members of your family? <u>I have a mom and a sister named Lela.</u> 2. What does your family like to do for fun? <u>We like to go hiking and camping together.</u> 3. What makes your family different than other families? <u>My family has all girls and no boys.</u>	How come all the families look a little bit different? Some families have no kids, some have a lot, and some have a little. Families today are also different than a long time ago.

Grades 3–5 Example (after reading)

Main Issue: <u>Traveling West</u>

Teacher Questions	My Questions/Thoughts
1. Why did people want to settle in the West? <u>They wanted to own land and have wide open spaces.</u> 2. What were some of the struggles for the pioneers moving west? <u>They had to face wild animals, little food, bad weather, and some dangerous Indians.</u> 3. How did many pioneers travel west? <u>Many used covered wagons to travel while others walked or rode horseback.</u>	I can't imagine what it would be like to walk for that many miles to get from one place to another. I think it would be scary to start over in a new land with no friends or stores to help me get settled. What happened if people got sick on the trail or out west? Did they have doctors?

Writing Strategies for Previewing and Reviewing in Social Studies *(cont.)*

Think Sheet *(cont.)*

Grades 6–8 Example (after reading)

Main Issue: ___Civil War___

Teacher Questions	My Questions/Thoughts
1. What were three of the causes of the Civil War? Slavery, States' Rights, and tariffs	Why did the United States fight itself? Why couldn't they work this out through talking?
2. How did the Civil War begin? Fort Sumter was fired upon and the battle began which led to more battles.	It seems like so many people died and for what reason?
3. What was an abolitionist? An abolitionist was a person who felt that slavery should be abolished and done away with immediately.	I read about families that had one son fighting for the North and one son fighting for the South. How can this happen? How was the Civil War resolved?

Name: _____

Think Sheet

Directions: Write your answers to the questions from your teacher. After the social studies reading assignment or activity, write any thoughts or questions that you have about the topic.

Main Issue: _____

Teacher Questions	My Questions/Thoughts

Writing Strategies for Previewing and Reviewing in Social Studies *(cont.)*

Free-Association Brainstorming

Background Information

The Free-Association Brainstorming strategy encourages divergent thinking for students and generates many ideas on a given subject. It also helps students access their prior knowledge on the subject being studied without requiring them to organize that information. Often, students have some content knowledge but are not prepared to organize it in a systematic fashion. This strategy is the beginning of the writing process.

Grade Levels/Standards Addressed

Grades 1–2 (Standard 1.1)
Grades 3–5 (Standard 1.1)
Grades 6–8 (Standard 1.1)

Genres

Expository, Narrative, Persuasive

Stages of Writing Process

Prewrite

Activity

Distribute copies of the Free-Association Brainstorming map (pages 59). Write the topic on the board, and have students write it at the center of the map. Do not discuss this topic or explain it. Instruct students to write in the surrounding circles any words, thoughts, ideas, or examples that come to mind. If there are too few circles, students can continue to add more. Next, meet as a class and share all the ideas that students came up with. Remind them that they may continue to think of

new ideas and can add them to their maps. The maps can be used as a springboard to writing or a way to access and/or organize prior knowledge on the subject being studied.

Variations

In primary grade classes, this activity is best completed as a class because it is meant to focus on the prewriting process of generating ideas—both good and bad—as quickly as possible. Write students' contributions on the board, so that writing will not hinder them. Use of the Free-Association Brainstorming map can be altered to fit the needs of the lesson and the students: It can be used independently (to assess each student's prior knowledge), in pairs or small groups (to generate additional ideas), or as a whole class (to allow for teacher prompting, modeling, or scaffolding).

Differentiation

Encourage ELLs to draw pictures or diagrams if that helps them more easily communicate their ideas. Challenge gifted students with a more complex concept that requires higher-order thinking skills. Have students who are writing and reading below grade level work with partners to assist in getting their ideas on paper. Remind them that the purpose is simply to get their ideas on paper without worrying about spelling or grammar.

Writing Strategies for Previewing and Reviewing in Social Studies *(cont.)*

Free-Association Brainstorming *(cont.)*

Grades 1–2 Example

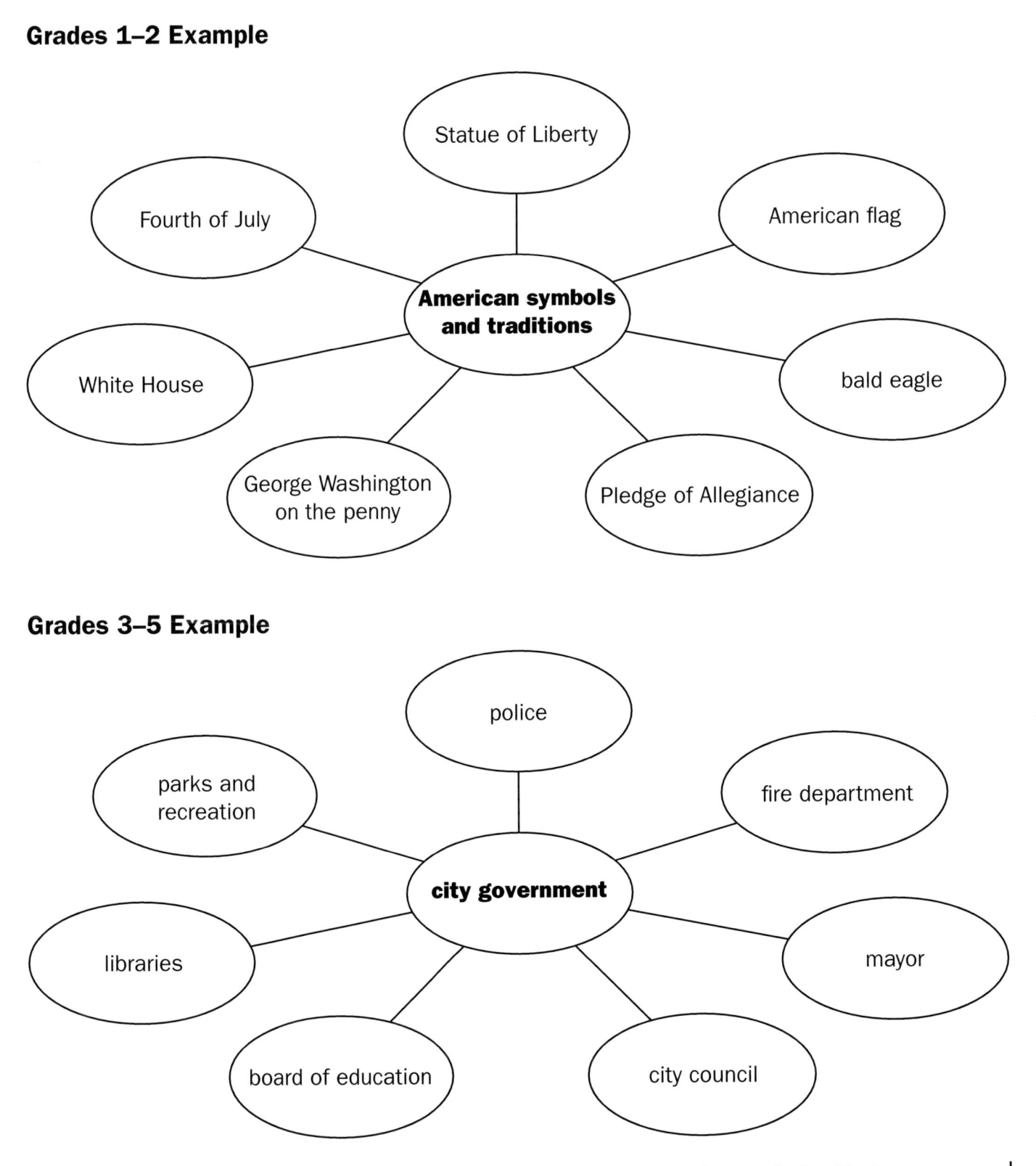

Grades 3–5 Example

Writing Strategies for Previewing and Reviewing in Social Studies *(cont.)*

Free-Association Brainstorming *(cont.)*

Grades 6–8 Example

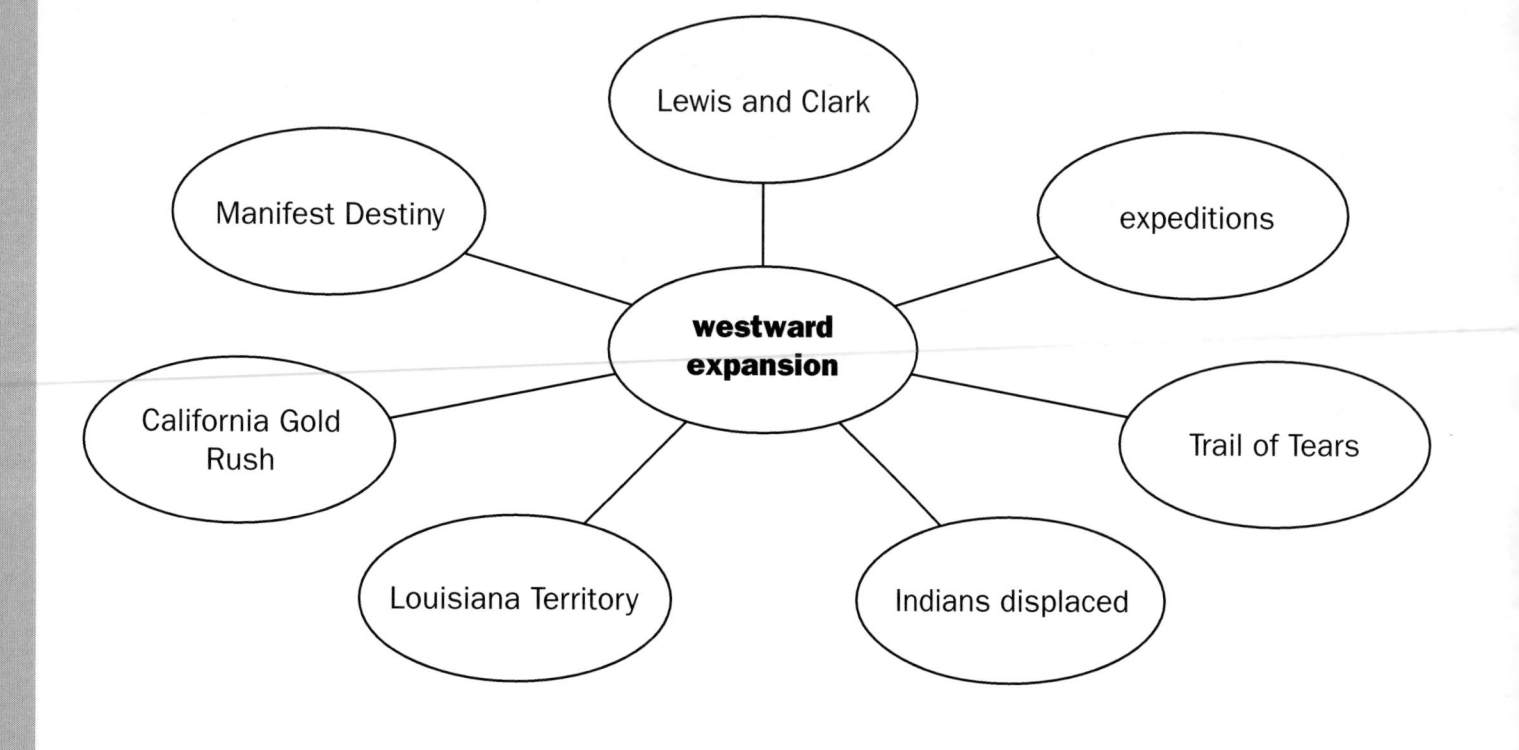

Name: _____

Free-Association Brainstorming

Directions: Write the topic in the center oval. Then add any words, thoughts, ideas, or examples in the surrounding ovals.

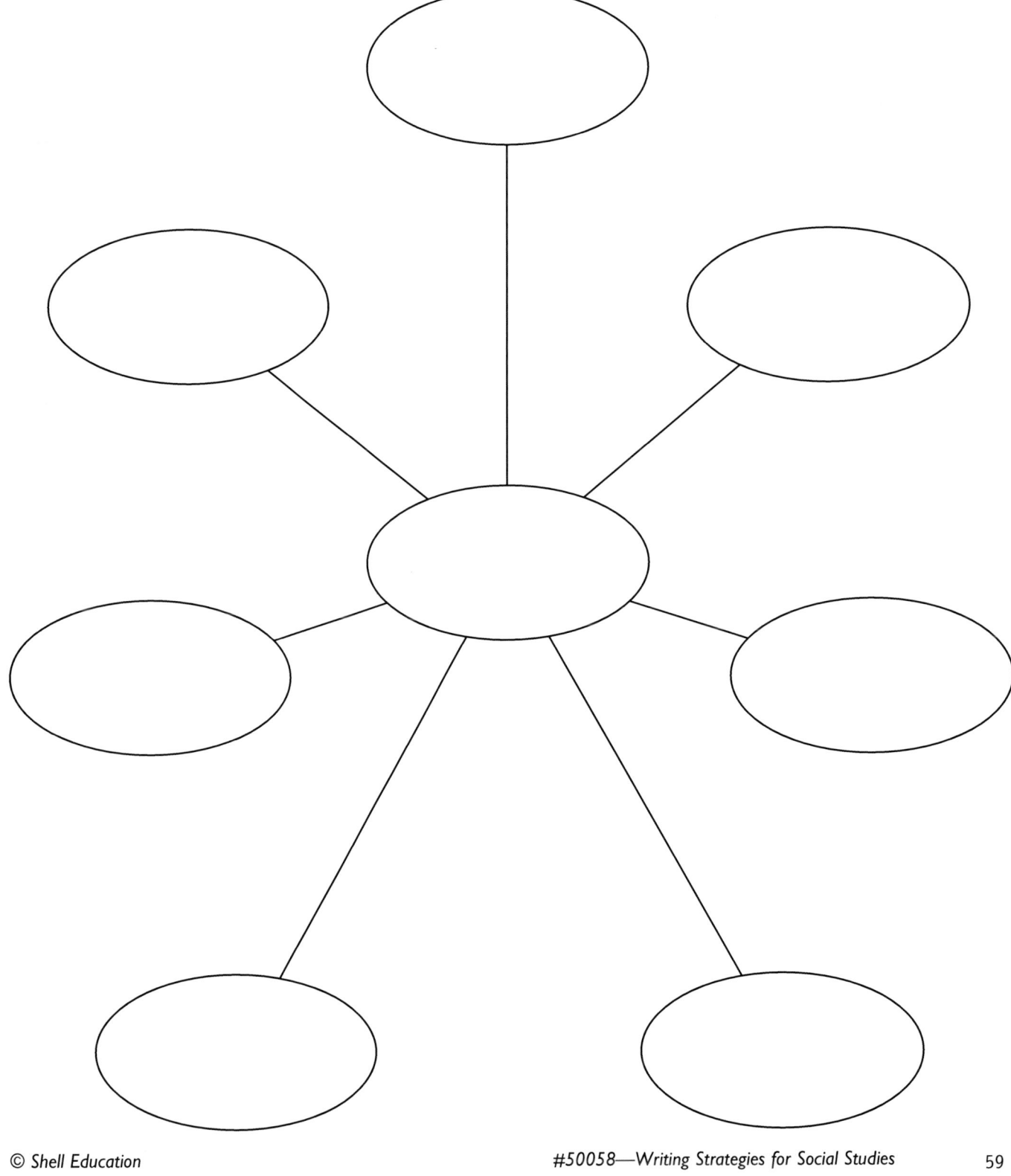

Writing Strategies for Previewing and Reviewing in Social Studies *(cont.)*

Probable Passages

Background Information

The Probable Passages strategy (Wood 1984) incorporates writing directly into a social studies lesson. This strategy is primarily used with basal readers but Readence, Bean, and Baldwin (1981) suggest that this strategy can be adapted for use with expository text. Its focus is to use key concepts or terms to make predictions about the content of a text. Students use key terms or concepts provided by the teacher to write short passages that could appear in the text. The goal is not necessarily to have their information correct the first time. The goal is to write using the types of language and sentence structure common to the genre and use the process of analyzing the information against a reliable source.

Grade Levels/Standards Addressed

Grades 1–2 (Standards 1.1–1.2)
Grades 3–5 (Standards 1.1–1.2)
Grades 6–8 (Standards 1.1–1.2)

Genres

Expository, Summary, Narrative, Persuasive

Stages of Writing Process

Prewrite, Draft, Revise

Activity

Before reading a selected social studies text, distribute the Probable Passages activity sheet (page 63). Introduce the topic and write the key vocabulary words on the board or overhead. Discuss the meanings of these words, and then call on students to define and use the words orally in sentences. Once students are familiar with the words, have them look for relationships among the words in the same way that writers look for related information while composing a rough draft. *Which word might be a main idea? Which words have common meanings or definitions? Which words go together? Which words are examples of another word?* You may want to construct a simple outline or diagram of how the words might be related as a quick prewriting scaffold. Then instruct students to write a short passage using the outline. There is no strict format to follow except that the key words must be utilized. Allow time for students to share their passages with partners or table team for feedback and input. After reading the selected social studies text, have students compare and contrast their Probable Passages with the text. This step is key because students are analyzing their own writing against published writing to verify information.

Differentiation

Provide clear, simple definitions and visuals of the key terms for ELLs to refer to as they write their paragraphs because it might be difficult for them to use complex terms they have just learned. Provide sentence frames and examples of how to write a paragraph for the ELLs as well. Instruct gifted students to write more than a paragraph or provide additional words for them to incorporate. Also, challenge them to write the passage and leave the key words blank then exchange with a partner to see if they can fill in the blanks. For students reading and writing below grade level, spend individual time in a writing conference working through the writing of the paragraph. Also, provide definitions for the key terms.

Writing Strategies for Previewing and Reviewing in Social Studies *(cont.)*

Probable Passages *(cont.)*

Grades 1–2 Example

Key Concepts:

farmers, workers, America, own, land, living, skills

Prewrite:

America, farmers and workers
    own land
    living, skills

Probable Passage:

Many of the people who came to America were farmers and workers. They wanted to own land to make a living. They had many skills.

How does your passage compare to the text?

My topic sentence includes farmers and workers, but the book's topic sentence only has farmers.

Grades 3–5 Example

Key Concepts:

Jamestown, ships, Chesapeake Bay, ocean, settlers

Prewrite:

Jamestown settlers
    ships, ocean
    Chesapeake Bay

Probable Passage:

The settlers moved to Jamestown. They came by ships across the ocean. They came to Chesapeake Bay.

How does your passage compare to the text?

My facts are correct, but I have very few details. That is probably because I didn't know much about the subject at first. Now, if I were to rewrite the passage, I would include many more details and more description about the colony.

Writing Strategies for Previewing and Reviewing in Social Studies *(cont.)*

Probable Passages *(cont.)*

Grades 6–8 Example

Key Concepts:

settlement, Daniel Boone, frontier, restless, cabin, rifle, supplies

Prewrite:

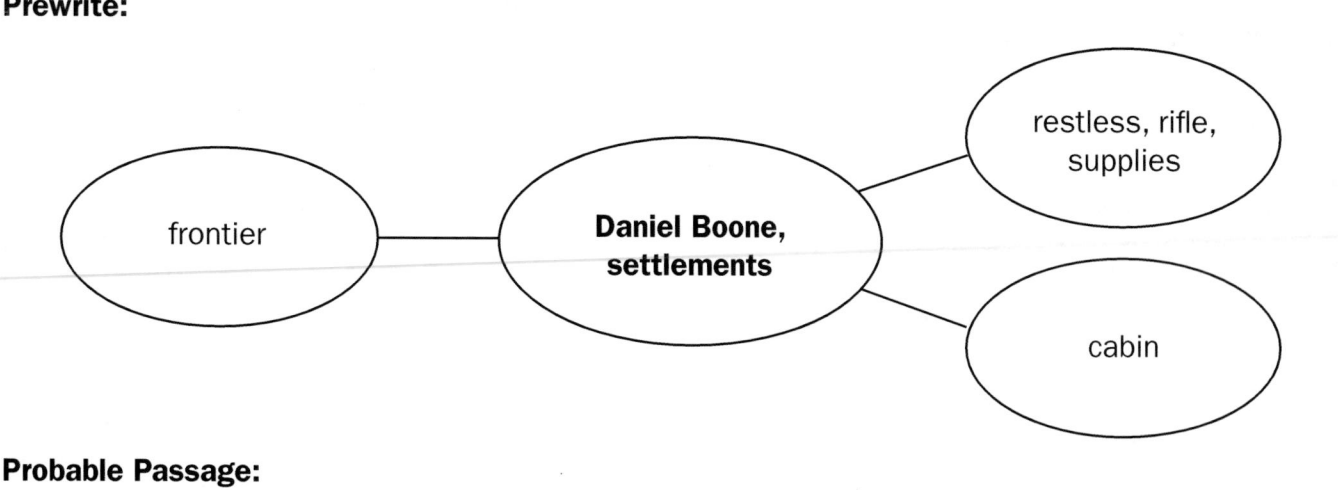

Probable Passage:

Daniel Boone liked to set up new settlements. He loved the frontier and exploring. He would get restless and take his rifle and supplies to go in search of wilderness. Each time he found a new place, he would have to build a new cabin.

How does your passage compare to the text?

Both paragraphs are about Daniel Boone. I'm surprised that most of my details were correct. I think next time, I would like to incorporate more vivid verbs and descriptive language to make my writing more interesting.

Name: _____

Probable Passages

Directions: Write down the key concepts for the lesson. Use a prewriting strategy and then write a probable passage using these words. After reading, compare your passage to the text.

Key Concepts:

_____

_____

Prewrite:

Probable Passage:

_____

_____

_____

_____

How does your passage compare to the text?

_____

_____

_____

_____

Writing Strategies for Previewing and Reviewing in Social Studies (cont.)

Guided Free Write

Background Information

The Guided Free Write strategy, introduced by Peter Elbow (1973), is a slight variation of free writing. The difference is that students are guided in the topics they write about instead of writing about whatever comes to mind. Using this strategy in a social studies class encourages students to write for a designated amount of time about observations, demonstrations, or experiments completed in class. It encourages students to record observations about what they are learning and thinking and to generate questions about social studies concepts. The Guided Free Write strategy allows students to practice writing using social studies terms and concepts. This builds confidence in writing, enhances vocabulary development, cements understanding, and leads to further discovery. This "thinking through" helps them clarify exactly what it is they do not understand. The primary focus is not on spelling, grammar, or mechanics. The intent is for students to think and write about their thinking.

Grade Levels/Standards Addressed

Grades 1–2 (Standard 1.8)
Grades 3–5 (Standard 1.5–1.6, 1.10)
Grades 6–8 (Standard 1.5)

Genres

Expository, Summary, Narrative, Persuasive

Stages of Writing Process

Draft

Activity

Prepare for the Guided Free Write by thinking of the central social studies concept or theme that is being taught and determine a question or questions that will generate thought about the subject. Using questions instead of just describing a concept encourages higher-order thinking. These questions can be controversial or may simply encourage students to think further on a given topic. To begin, write the question on the board and instruct students to write on this topic in a notebook or on a piece of paper. Here are some suggestions for using Guided Free Writes:

- Be sure that all students have access to paper and pencils, so they can spend the entire time thinking and writing.

- Tell students not to cross out any information but rather to continually add to their writing. There are no bad ideas. Many of these beginning thoughts will lead to new ideas or trails of thought.

- Keep the classroom free of distractions and noise so that students can focus on their writing.

- Set a timer for 10–20 minutes. This may differ depending on the age of the students and the purpose of the Guided Free Write. Remind students that if they are actively thinking on the topic, then it is okay to pause in their writing.

- Remind students not to focus on spelling, grammar, or punctuation. The focus is about getting ideas on paper.

Writing Strategies for Previewing and Reviewing in Social Studies *(cont.)*

Guided Free Write *(cont.)*

Variations

Allow students in the primary grades to draw pictures along with writing or typing to explain their thoughts. You may choose to have some students complete the Guided Free Write on the computer. Both typing on the computer and writing on paper provides the student with informal writing experience.

Differentiation

Allow ELLs to write words or phrases or draw pictures related to what they are thinking about. Provide sentence frames to model how to begin the answers. Encourage ELLs to put concepts down on paper and not to worry about correct tense or wording. Have them share their free writing with you in order to bring voice to what they have written or drawn. Coach gifted students to write about higher-level concepts or processes. The more complex the concept, the more questions, concerns, and solutions will be generated. For students reading and writing below grade level, provide time for discussion before writing to build their confidence. Also allow these students to use pictures, words, phrases, etc., if necessary, instead of writing complete sentences and paragraphs.

Writing Strategies for Previewing and Reviewing in Social Studies *(cont.)*

Guided Free Write *(cont.)*

Grades 1–2 Example

Question:

What are the different jobs that people hold in our community?

Student Free Write:

Firefighters put out fires and keep people safe. Teachers teach kids how to read and write and do math. Police officers make sure that everyone follows the laws. Sometimes they have to take people to jail.

Grades 3–5 Example

Question:

What do you think it would be like to have grown up as a slave?

Student Free Write:

I'm sure it would have been very hard work. Slave children had to work hard, picking cotton in the fields, working in the fields, carrying heavy buckets of water from the well to the house, doing chores around the plantation, or working in the kitchen. I guess maybe I would have gotten used to the hard work, but it would have been terrible to have a family member sold away to another owner. I can't imagine how it would have felt to have my own sister sold away, and to never see her again. That would have been the most difficult part, I think.

Writing Strategies for Previewing and Reviewing in Social Studies *(cont.)*

Guided Free Write *(cont.)*

Grades 6–8 Example

Question:

Do you think the American Indians were treated fairly in Early America?

Student Free Write:

I believe the treatment that American Indians received was unfair and criminal. The settlers came in to inhabited land, bringing disease and dangers to the native people. Although there were times of peace and respect between the two groups, the American Indians were ultimately overtaken by the European settlers. Their land was taken, and they were forced to move to harsher lands. Some were forced to give up their religion and adopt a more European way of life, in effect giving up their own culture.

Writing Strategies for Previewing and Reviewing in Social Studies (cont.)

End-of-Class Reflection

Background Information

With the End of Class Reflection, students write on a note card the two or three most important things learned from a reading assignment, social studies activity, observation, or demonstration, as well as two or three questions they want to ask about the central topic. This strategy meets many social studies classroom needs: Students have an opportunity to summarize and glean the main concepts, articulate their learning, and ask questions of the teacher. Teachers are able to quickly assess student understanding and analyze student reflections to direct future lessons. Research shows that writing about learning is a key way to create lifelong learning.

Grade Levels/Standards Addressed

Grades 1–2 (Standard 1.6)
Grades 3–5 (Standard 1.10–1.11)
Grades 6–8 (Standard 1.12)

Genres

Expository

Stages of Writing Process

Draft

Activity

At the end of a given social studies lesson, instruct students to write down three key things they learned during the lesson and three questions they still have about the topic. This activity can be completed in a student journal or on a 3x5 card that can be collected for teacher review.

Variation

For younger students who are still learning to write, consider recording students' dictated responses on the board. With upper grades, ask students to rank their key points in order of priority or emphasis, then lead a brief discussion to review key concepts, analyze rankings, and discuss any questions that were raised.

Differentiation

Allow ELLs to write words, phrases, or draw pictures to explain their key points or questions. Encourage them to get concepts down on paper and not worry about correct verb tense or wording. Expect gifted students to write more than three key points or to write an analysis of the learning they gathered from the lesson. Encourage these students to write questions that are open-ended and encourage higher-level thinking. For students reading and writing below grade level, provide time—perhaps in a Think-Pair-Share—for discussion before writing. If students have an opportunity to discuss what they have learned, it will be easier for them to write. Model a sample response, or simply the beginning of a sample response, to show students how to get started. Then ask them to use the model to write down their own thoughts.

Writing Strategies for Previewing and Reviewing in Social Studies *(cont.)*

End-of-Class Reflection *(cont.)*

Grades 1–2 Example

Learning:

I learned that being a firefighter is dangerous.

Firefighters work for the city.

Firefighters have to have training before they can fight fires.

Questions:

How does a fire get started?

Why can't people just get out of fire before they die?

How do dogs help firefighters?

Grades 3–5 Example

Learning:

Women ran the farms when the men went off to fight the Civil War.

Women worked as spies during the war.

I learned in class about some women serving as nurses and even as doctors.

Questions:

Why don't we hear more about women in the history books?

How did the North and South learn to work together after fighting so much?

How many women died during the Civil War?

Writing Strategies for Previewing and Reviewing in Social Studies *(cont.)*

End-of-Class Reflection *(cont.)*

Grades 6–8 Example

Learning:

The Cold War was not a war at all.

The Cold War was a build up of weapons.

The USSR and the US were ready to fight each other.

Questions:

What kept countries from using nuclear weapons?

What happened to all of the nuclear weapons?

How many people died during the cold war from being exposed to nuclear weapons?

Writing Strategies for Previewing and Reviewing in Social Studies *(cont.)*

Reader–Response Writing Chart

Background Information

The Reader-Response Writing Chart strategy, introduced by Carey-Webb (2001), asks students to think about what they bring to a reading passage and what the author of the text brings to the passage. When writing expository social studies pieces, students need to try to remain neutral and focus on facts, data, or research. In contrast, when writing persuasive pieces in social studies, students must establish a clear point of view. This strategy helps students become more aware of their biases and in what types of writing it is appropriate to use them.

Grade Levels/Standards Addressed

Grades 3–5 (Standard 1.4, 1.10–1.11)
Grades 6–8 (Standard 1.4, 1.12)

Genres

Expository, Narrative, Persuasive

Stages of Writing Process

Draft

Activity

After reading a selected social studies text, distribute copies of the Reader-Response Writing Chart (page 73). On the left side of the page, students write down the author's point of view on the topic as well as any examples of bias or prejudice. For older students, require them to cite examples from the text to support their ideas. On the right side of the page, students record the bias or prejudice that they had going into the reading.

Discuss the following questions with the students:

- What do you know about the subject?
- What are your feelings about this topic?
- Have you read anything about this subject before?
- What did you think about this subject?
- What tone does the author use in the text?
- Can you tell what he or she is thinking?
- Do you think the author has preconceptions about the topic?

In conclusion, ask students to record whether or not their views or opinions changed after reading.

Variation

For primary grade classes, recreate the Reader-Response Writing Chart on the board or a large piece of chart paper. Lead a class discussion about each question and allow students to help formulate responses to add to the chart.

Differentiation

Encourage ELLs to work with partners when using this strategy to lower anxiety levels and promote collaboration. These students can record answers and share in the discussion. Challenge gifted students to identify examples from the text to support their views of the author's bias and prejudice. Ask them to write about how these influence the author's writing. Then challenge them to write a synthesis of what they have learned. Take time to define and provide examples of bias and prejudice in a level-appropriate text for students reading and writing below grade level.

Writing Strategies for Previewing and Reviewing in Social Studies *(cont.)*

Reader-Response Writing Chart *(cont.)*

Grades 3–5 Example

The Author	Me
Some people felt that slavery was good while others felt that it was terrible. The country couldn't decide what to do about this issue. States were divided.	I think slavery is terrible. I think that it is never right and it is worth fighting a war over. How can any human being ever think it is okay?

Grades 6–8 Example

The Author	Me
Mountain Men traveled all over the Northwest part of the United States long before the settlers arrived. The settlement in Oregon did not begin until 1834. The Oregon Trail led the way to the Northwest and wagons began to come.	I think Mountain Men were settlers. They should be given credit for being the first settlers of an area. They may not have built homes but they lived there first. They knew the area better than anyone.

Name: _____

Reader-Response Writing Chart

Directions: On the left side of the chart, write down the author's point of view on the topic. Also, note any examples of prejudice or bias. On the right side, record your own point of view regarding the subject.

The Author	Me

Using Journals in Social Studies

Benefits of Journal Writing

The quote, "How do I know what I think until I see what I say?" by novelist E. M. Forster makes journal writing extremely relevant to students in the social studies class. Even in this crowded, technological world, there is still room for personal writing. Being able to express personal feelings in writing will always be vital to making sense of this world. Journal writing in social studies allows the writer to use words to express his or her understanding of social studies concepts and how these concepts relate to the real world.

There are many benefits to using journal-writing strategies in the social studies classroom. Journal writing provides a means for the student to absorb the complex processes, vague concepts, and large amounts of information presented in social studies. Journal writing is a way for students to sort out all the new information. Writing about what they are learning helps students make sense of it. By writing in a daily journal, students become more comfortable with and confident in their writing and increase the number of words they are writing. This is another way for students to see their writing progress.

Journals mean different things to different educators, and they are used for a variety of purposes. However, the support for journal writing seems almost universal. Many different types of journal-writing exercises can be incorporated into the social studies classroom. Yinger (1985) states that "writing is a powerful tool for learning as well as for communicating" (p. 31).

How to Implement Journal Writing

Incorporating journal writing into the social studies class is easy because it does not take much class time and there is little or no teacher preparation. Journals do not need to be graded; the focus is on content, not on students' writing abilities or spelling, grammar, and punctuation skills. Be sure that the students feel positive about writing each day in their journal. Do not make it seem like a punishment; your attitude as a teacher will mean everything.

Create or designate a social studies journal for each student—and you—to use regularly. Students should date each entry so that it becomes a written record, documenting their growth and progress in learning. Be sure students have notebooks and pencils ready at journal time so that they can spend the entire time writing, instead of looking for materials. Model good writing behavior by writing in your own journal.

Set aside a specific time each day during class for journal writing. Be sure to allow enough time for students to write a meaningful entry but not so much that it becomes boring and tedious. Select certain days throughout the week to have students share their journal entries with one another.

Journal-Writing Strategies for Social Studies

Vocabulary Journal

Background Information

The Vocabulary Journal provides an opportunity for students to communicate, and it can lead to self-reflection and growth. The Vocabulary Journal is an excellent resource for the social studies classroom because it allows students to write personally about the words they are learning in social studies. The entries in a Vocabulary Journal vary—each one meets a specific need or skill. Expectations for the writing in the Vocabulary Journal vary according to students' levels.

Grade Levels/Standards Addressed

Grades 1–2 (Standard 1.8)
Grades 3–5 (Standard 1.5–1.6)
Grades 6–8 (Standard 1.5)

Genres

Expository, Narrative

Stages of Writing Process

Draft

Activity

Designate or create a notebook for each student to use as a Vocabulary Journal. This journal helps the student keep track of and reflect on the many new words that are introduced in the social studies curriculum. Following are a variety of strategies to use with the Vocabulary Journal:

- Log social studies vocabulary words and their definitions, as well as synonyms, antonyms, comparisons, etc.

- Write about the words students are learning. Ask students: *What has the experience been like? What have you learned? What do you hope to remember? What strategies can you use to retain these words? How does learning the meanings of words help you better understand social studies concepts and information?*

- Explain the strategies that can be used when students encounter an unfamiliar word.

- Create a piece of fiction, such as a letter or story, using the new social studies vocabulary words.

- Write sentences using the vocabulary words.

- List the resources that are available for students to use when researching new vocabulary words.

- Design a journal entry to be shared with a partner or small group.

Variation

For primary grade students, create a "class" Vocabulary Journal. Allow students to dictate entries to be recorded by the teacher. This provides an opportunity for the teacher to model good writing skills. Or, provide students with their own journals and allow them to draw and label pictures of vocabulary words. If students are able to use the word in a sentence or explain what it means orally, then challenge them to write their response in their journals.

Journal-Writing Strategies for Social Studies *(cont.)*

Vocabulary Journal *(cont.)*

Differentiation

Select Vocabulary Journal strategies that will encourage growth for ELLs, but not overwhelm them, such as recording new vocabulary terms with their definitions, synonyms, examples, etc. Remind them to draw pictures to help create a visual connection. Challenge gifted students to write about complex social studies terms in their Vocabulary Journals. Allow them to select words and entries that they are personally interested in. Limit the number of vocabulary words that students reading and writing below grade level write about. Provide them with sentence frames to help them meet the expectations of the assigned activity.

Journal-Writing Strategies
for Social Studies *(cont.)*

Vocabulary Journal *(cont.)*

Grades 1–2 Example

Vocabulary Words

1. **document**—a piece of writing that tells about something

2. **artifact**—something that people used a long time ago that tells about their lives

Grades 3–5 Example

What strategies can I use when I come across a word I do not know? There are many things that I can do. One thing I can do is look at the other words in the sentence to see if there are clues that can help me. Sometimes I recognize parts of the word, such as a prefix, suffix, or root, and I can use those to help me figure out what the word means. If I'm lucky, the author used apposition, and the definition is right there in the sentence. If none of those strategies work, I can look up the unfamiliar word in a dictionary or in a thesaurus.

Journal-Writing Strategies for Social Studies *(cont.)*

Vocabulary Journal *(cont.)*

Grades 6–8 Example

1. **tyranny**—absolute power by a single ruler

2. **oligarchy**—government by the few

3. **democracy**—government by the people, rule of the majority

4. **dictatorship**—absolute power with one person or clique

similar to tyranny or

oligarchy

Journal-Writing Strategies
for Social Studies *(cont.)*

Dialogue Journal

Background Information

A Dialogue Journal (Staton 1980) is just what the name implies—a dialogue between two or more people. Dialogue Journals can be shared between a student and a teacher or between one student and another student (Goldsmith 1995). This strategy does entail more work for teachers, but the dialogue exchange and extra effort is rewarding and informative. Using this strategy, teachers can recognize areas of student concern or misunderstanding with respect to the social studies content, as well as student progress in communicating thoughts and ideas in writing. Students benefit from having an audience for their writing and frequent opportunities for using writing as an authentic form of communication.

Grade Levels/Standards Addressed

Grades 1–2 (Standard 1.6)
Grades 3–5 (Standard 1.5, 1.10)
Grades 6–8 (Standard 1.5)

Genres

Narrative

Stages of Writing Process

Draft

Activity

Designate a notebook or binder to be used as the social studies Dialogue Journal. Ask students to respond to a prompt or question, or occasionally allow them to write about a topic of their own. Using a combination of both adds variety to the strategy. Students should exchange Dialogue Journals with the teacher or a peer, who then reads the journal entry and responds to questions or adds comments. Then exchange again and write a new entry to continue the dialogue.

Variation

Create a teacher-class Dialogue Journal for primary grade students. Or, provide a question or prompt with a frame for the answer to assist these students.

Differentiation

Remind ELLs that this is a personal assignment, so they can respond in a way that is comfortable for them. Allow them to choose how they would like to communicate. Challenge gifted students by giving them specific feedback that will stimulate challenging thoughts and ideas and develop more effective writing skills. Encourage them to research ideas further and write about their findings in the next journal entry. When dialoguing with students reading and writing below grade level, be sure to keep your writing clear, concise, and easy to read and model correct spelling. Use the journal as an opportunity to challenge their thinking even if the reading or writing skills are not high. Carefully consider with whom to pair these students when students exchange with each other.

Journal-Writing Strategies for Social Studies (cont.)

Dialogue Journal (cont.)

Grades 1–2 Example

Student: Why did they make kids work on the farm a long time ago?

Teacher: That's a really good question. Families back then did not have very much money. They needed their children to help make money to buy food. Children worked in factories or on the family farm. Rules keeping kids from working didn't happen for many years.

Student: I think I would like to gather the eggs from the chickens. Also, it would be fun to pick the fruit in the orchards. But I would not like to clean up after the animals!

Teacher: I agree! It would not have been fun to clean up after the animals. But everyone in the family had to help on the farm. That was how the family earned money.

Grades 3–5 Example

Student: Today we learned about the equal rights for women. Why did it take so long for women to get the right to vote?

Teacher: Changes like that can take a very long time. Many people, some women included, did not think that women were smart enough to make decisions about voting. Many women were also illiterate and did not know how to read or write. I think some men were also afraid to give women power because they were afraid of what might happen if they did. Now that women have the right to vote, why do you think many women still don't vote?

 #50058—*Writing Strategies for Social Studies*

Journal-Writing Strategies
for Social Studies (cont.)

Dialogue Journal (cont.)

Grades 6–8 Example

Student:	Making the decision to use the atomic bomb in World War II was a difficult one. Why on earth was it ever used?
Teacher:	This was a very difficult decision to make. Part of the reasons to use the bomb had to do with the fact the United States was just coming off a huge battle in Europe. The armies were depleted and tired.
Student:	Perhaps the U.S. government saw using the atomic bomb as a quick way to exercise force and end the war quickly. I suppose there are always pros and cons to every decision we make.
Teacher:	That would make an interesting analysis. What do you think the pros were in that decision? What were the cons?

Journal-Writing Strategies for Social Studies *(cont.)*

Highlighted Journal

Background Information

The Highlighted Journal is a strategy that assists students in making connections with their learning. Students need to write regularly in their journals for at least a month before trying this strategy. Students read through their journals and highlight key points—significant information or discoveries, points from class discussions, or concepts from a social studies text. This strategy helps develop research skills by asking students to analyze their written work for trends, commonalities, main ideas, themes, etc., which are crucial to the scientific inquiry process as well as to the prewriting stage of the writing process.

Grade Levels/Standards Addressed

Grades 1–2 (Standard 1.1)
Grades 3–5 (Standard 1.1, 4.1)
Grades 6–8 (Standard 1.1, 4.3)

Genres

Expository

Stages of Writing Process

Prewrite

Activity

Give students frequent, regular opportunities to write in their journals, so that they will have enough writing to analyze. Tell them to read through their journals, looking for key words or concepts, common themes or interesting points.

Provide highlighter markers or allow students to use pencils to underline key points in their journal entries. Ask them to share their highlighted selections and the reasons they chose them with each other or with the class.

Variation

For a primary grade class using a single journal between the teacher and the class, read through the journal entries together and ask students to identify the key points to highlight.

Differentiation

Prompt ELLs to look for common words that they see throughout their journals, as these are likely some of the key concepts and important vocabulary words that they need to know. Using this strategy serves as an effective review tool for them. Consider having gifted students explain to the class how they chose their highlighted points. For students reading and writing below grade level, take time to explicitly model how to identify significant information or common ideas in your own journal before asking them to apply the strategy.

Journal-Writing Strategies
for Social Studies *(cont.)*

Highlighted Journal *(cont.)*

Grades 1–2 Example

Nov. 2

<u>Covered wagons</u> were used to travel across the plains. <u>Oxen</u> were the animals used to pull the <u>wagons</u>. Some people used <u>handcarts</u> to travel with.

Nov. 4

Some people didn't have <u>wagons</u>. They <u>carried</u> things on their backs. They had to bring what they needed.

Nov. 5

Everyone had to <u>walk</u>. The trip took a few months. Some people <u>died</u> on the trip.

Grades 3–5 Example

Feb. 10

<u>Abraham Lincoln</u> was <u>opposed</u> to <u>slavery</u>. He felt that no human should ever have a master. On the other hand, Lincoln was not an <u>abolitionist</u>. An <u>abolitionist</u> felt that <u>slavery</u> should be abolished everywhere.

Feb. 11

<u>Abraham Lincoln</u> knew that the federal government didn't have the right to change the way the laws were set up in the southern states.

Feb. 13

<u>Lincoln</u> wanted to make sure that all new states added to the union would be "free" states. He issued the <u>Emancipation Proclamation</u> on Jan. 1, 1863. This freed all <u>slaves</u> in the rebelling states.

Journal-Writing Strategies
for Social Studies *(cont.)*

Highlighted Journal *(cont.)*

Grades 6–8 Example

Jan. 8

In the <u>Compact of 1802</u>, <u>Georgia</u> gave up its western <u>territory</u> because the <u>U.S. government</u> promised to get <u>Georgia</u> control of the <u>Indian tribal lands</u>.

Jan. 10

The <u>Cherokees</u> agreed to the <u>Treaty of New Echota</u> to be relocated. The <u>U.S. government</u> was supposed to pay them 4.5 million dollars to remove themselves. The <u>Cherokees</u> and some white Americans were opposed to the treaty.

Jan. 11

<u>President Van Buren</u> sent 7,000 troops to <u>New Echota</u> in <u>Georgia</u> to round up the <u>Cherokees</u>. About 17,000 <u>Cherokees</u> were taken to camps at gunpoint.

Jan. 12

About 4,000 <u>Cherokees</u> died on the "<u>Trail of Tears</u>". It was 1,200-mile journey from Tennessee or Alabama to the Indian Territory.

Journal-Writing Strategies for Social Studies *(cont.)*

Key Phrase Journal

Background Information

The Key Phrase Journal (Bringle and Hatcher 1996) is a strategy that assists students in regularly incorporating new social studies vocabulary and phrases into their writing. During a social studies lesson, the teacher selects a list of social studies terms students are to use in a journal entry. By using this strategy on a regular basis, students can develop a more solid understanding of the social studies terms and become more adept at using them in writing. This strategy is most commonly used with a reading selection, but it can also be used when conducting a social studies experiment or observation activity.

Grade Levels/Standards Addressed

Grades 1–2 (Standard 1.2)
Grades 3–5 (Standard 1.2)
Grades 6–8 (Standard 1.2)

Genres

Expository, Persuasive

Stages of Writing Process

Draft

Activity

Prior to teaching a social studies lesson, make a list of words or phrases that students should understand thoroughly. Throughout the reading lesson or activity, introduce the words and use them in sentences or point them out in the text. Discuss the meanings of the words with students. After the lesson, or later in the day, write the list of words and phrases on the board and instruct students to write an entry in their journals using those words.

Variation

With primary grade students, create sentences orally as a class. Write the sentences on the board or invite students to write them. To challenge upper grade students, let them select the words to incorporate into the journal entries, and ask them to persuade you to agree with their choices.

Differentiation

For ELLs, select from the list only the terms with which they are somewhat familiar—words that have been discussed as a class and defined on numerous occasions. Have them use only those words in their Key Phrase Journal so that they are not frustrated. Challenge gifted students to use words that are more difficult or less familiar to them by researching the terms and determining ways to incorporate them into the journal entry. For students reading and writing below grade level, allow them to select only one or two words to use in their journal entry and to use resources to look up these words, if needed.

Journal-Writing Strategies
for Social Studies _(cont.)_

Key Phrase Journal _(cont.)_

Grades 1–2 Example

Key Words:

symbols, flag, bald eagle, Statue of Liberty, Liberty Bell

Journal Entry:

There are many symbols of our country. Our flag is red, white, and blue. The bald eagle is our national bird. The Statue of Libery is in New York. The Liberty Bell has a crack in it.

Grades 3–5 Example

Key Words:

Appomattox Court House, Civil War, surrender, McLean's House, Battle of Bull Run

Journal Entry:

Appomattox Court House is a very important town in our state. The Battle of Bull Run, which was the first battle of the Civil War, took place just a few miles north. General Lee surrendered to General Grant at McLean's House. This ended the Civil War.

Journal-Writing Strategies
for Social Studies *(cont.)*

Key Phrase Journal *(cont.)*

Grades 6–8 Example

Key Words:

Code of Hammurabi, gods, rules, punishments, preserved, Babylonia, ancient times

Journal Entry:

The Code of Hammurabi is one of the best-preserved sets of laws from ancient times. It lists the rules of the Babylonian society. The punishments ranged from small fines to death. Hammurabi wrote the set of laws to please the gods.

Journal-Writing Strategies for Social Studies (cont.)

Double-Entry Journal

Background Information

The Double-Entry Journal (Angelo and Cross 1993) is a strategy to help students summarize what they read and to connect the reading with their own words and understanding. A Double-Entry Journal has two columns: one for notes, paraphrasing, and summaries of the social studies reading, and the other for entries that express students' thoughts in their own words. This strategy allows teachers to immediately gauge student comprehension of the objectives and use that information in future lessons. It also focuses on the prewriting skills of note-taking and information analysis. Students analyze, synthesize, question, and write about what they are reading as well as personalize and reflect on what they have learned.

Grade Levels/Standards Addressed

Grades 3–5 (Standard 1.10–1.11)
Grades 6–8 (Standard 1.12)

Genres

Expository, Narrative, Persuasive

Stages of Writing Process

Prewrite

Activity

Before reading a selected social studies text, distribute Double-Entry Journal pages (page 90). On the left side, have students write notes from or summaries of the reading, and on the right side have them record personal reflections, observations, or questions. Select passages to focus on content or clarify misunderstandings, or allow students to select their own passages because of particular interest or questions they have about them. When students have completed both sides of their journal entries, have them draw arrows to show the connections and relationships between the summary of the content and their personal thoughts and reflections. This reinforces for students what they are learning.

Differentiation

For ELLs, scaffold the activity by providing notes and key concepts for the left column in simple sentences that are easy to understand. Have these students read and discuss the notes before writing about them. Once they have written the personal reflection, suggest that ELLs draw arrows to show connections between the notes and their own words. Challenge gifted students to write what they are thinking about as they write their notes. Another term for this is "thinking aloud." Once the note-taking, summarizing, and "thinking aloud" is completed, have them write personal reflections. For students reading and writing below grade level, have them focus on only one or two key points to summarize from the lesson. Instruct them to keep their notes brief and limited so they can focus on their personal reflection without being overwhelmed by too many concepts to discuss.

Journal-Writing Strategies for Social Studies *(cont.)*

Double-Entry Journal *(cont.)*

Grades 3–5 Example

Title: **The Alamo**

Text Passage	Student Response
"In the 1830s, the Mexican government tried to tighten its rule over Texas. This angered the Texans. In 1835, fighting broke out between Mexican soldiers and Texans."	A few years ago I went to the Alamo. It is interesting to read about the facts and what happened there. I can picture the whole thing in my mind.

Reference: Silver Burdett & Ginn. 1991. Texans are defeated at the Alamo. In *Our country people in time and place*, 374. Morristown, NJ: Silver Burdett & Ginn.

Grades 6–8 Example

Title: **World War I Begins**

Text Passage	Student Response
"Soon after World War I started, President Woodrow Wilson declared that the United States would remain neutral. You'll remember that a neutral country is one that stays out of a war."	Why doesn't the United States remain neutral in wars today? It seems like the U.S. gets involved in more wars than they need to. Why?

Reference: Silver Burdett & Ginn. 1991. The United States is drawn into war. In *Our country people in time and place*, 524. Morristown, NJ: Silver Burdett & Ginn.

Name: _____

Double-Entry Journal

Title: _____

Text Passage	Student Response
• Write the passage directly from the text. • Write notes from the text. • Write a summary of a section of text.	• What are your reactions to the text? • What does it remind you of? • What questions do you still have?

Journal-Writing Strategies for Social Studies *(cont.)*

Critical Incident Journal

Background Information

The Critical Incident Journal (Bringle and Hatcher 1996) focuses on a specific event that occurred in class. The critical incident will be different for each student. Examples of critical incidents in a social studies class may include the results of a photo analysis, an "aha! moment" when a student finally understood the material, the confusing part of a lesson, a low test grade, a reaction to a social studies simulation, or another type of personal experience. This quick writing strategy provides a springboard for future writing or research activities.

Grade Levels/Standards Addressed

Grades 1–2 (Standard 1.6)
Grades 3–5 (Standard 1.8, 1.10)
Grades 6–8 (Standard 1.7–1.8)

Genres

Expository, Narrative

Stages of Writing Process

Draft

Activity

Prior to teaching a social studies lesson, explain that students should look for a critical incident throughout the course of a lesson. Describe a critical incident and give examples. Explain that students should identify the critical incident during the lesson and be prepared to write about it in their journals. Here are some questions to consider:

- What is the significant event you would like to write about in your journal?
- Why is this event important to you?

- What was your favorite or least favorite part of the lesson today?
- Describe the event. What happened?
- What did you learn from this experience?
- How does this fit in with what you are learning in social studies class?

Variation

For grades 1–2, invite students to draw and label their critical incidents and display the drawings on the social studies board. Those who are able can then write sentences to explain their choice of critical incidents. This strategy may be especially meaningful following a social studies simulation.

Differentiation

For ELLs, create a shared experience during the class that they can discuss with other students, such as conducting a class vote, panning for gold, or role-playing the Boston Tea Party. After students have had time to discuss this experience, allow time for students to write in their journals. Ask gifted students to write about their critical incident in a specific genre: Use vivid imagery and descriptive language to describe the critical incident, use persuasive language to show why the incident is the most critical, or compare and contrast the critical incident with a previous one. Also, encourage gifted students to identify critical incidents, such as trends in population growth or major political developments, in newspapers or other resources. Provide examples of the critical incident journal for students reading and writing below grade level. Also, allow them to work with partners to discuss events during the social studies lesson, so they feel more confident about writing about them.

Journal-Writing Strategies
for Social Studies *(cont.)*

Critical Incident Journal *(cont.)*

Grades 1–2 Example

The best day in social studies for me was when we went on a trip to the Historical Family Farm. We got to see the way people lived many years ago. I think it looked like a lot of fun. I would have loved wearing a dress and a bonnet and taking care of the animals. The food was all cooked on a fire. The family had many pets like cows, horses, sheep, and chickens.

Grades 3–5 Example

We watched a movie in social studies today that was really good. We watched a movie about the Lusitania. The Lusitania was a passenger ship that was traveling to the United States during the time of World War I. The ship was hit by German torpedoes and it sunk quickly into the sea. Over 1200 people were killed and many of them were U.S. citizens. I was amazed to watch the footage. It was unbelievable. It reminded me of what happened in our country on 9/11.

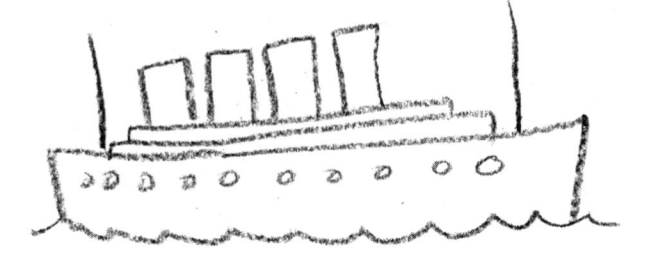

Journal-Writing Strategies
for Social Studies (cont.)

Critical Incident Journal (cont.)

Grades 6–8 Example

Today we had a guest speaker in social studies come talk about the way that Indians were treated in the late 1800s. The speaker explained that the Apaches were the last group of Indians that refused to be put on a reservation. They lived in the southwest. Geronimo attacked the white settlements. They were able to keep hidden from the United States troops for 10 years. That is amazing to me. It must have been very difficult for these Indians. They finally captured Geronimo and forced him to surrender. The Apaches had to move to a reservation.

Journal-Writing Strategies for Social Studies *(cont.)*

Three-Part Journal

Background Information

The Three-Part Journal (Bringle and Hatcher 1996) asks students to divide the journal page into thirds. On a weekly basis, students are asked to write in their Three-Part Journals.

Grade Levels/Standards Addressed

Grades 1–2 (Standard 1.6, 1.8)
Grades 3–5 (Standard 1.5–1.6, 1.10)
Grades 6–8 (Standard 1.5, 1.8)

Genres

Expository, Narrative

Stages of Writing Process

Draft

Activity

Designate or create a notebook for students to use for the Three-Part Journal (page 97). Primary grade teachers may want to use this strategy as a class until students are able to complete it independently. In the first section, students describe insights that they gained from the lesson. Questions to prompt students might include:

- What was your favorite part?
- What do you think about what you have learned?

In the second section, students write about how this new information or experience fits in with what they already know. Ask students to explain what they knew previously about this topic, and then show what new information they have learned. Ask questions such as these to prompt students:

- What did you already know about this topic?
- What new information did you learn?
- How does the "new" information fit in with the "old" information?

In the last section, students write about how the new knowledge relates or can be applied to their personal lives. This will vary, as each student will apply the social studies material in a different way. Consider writing some prompts on the board:

- How might you relate this new learning to your life?
- How does this information change your views of the topic?
- How might you use this information in your own life?

Finally, allow time for students to share what they have written.

Differentiation

Explain the different sections of the journal page to ELLs to ensure that they understand the purpose of each section. Model how to complete the journal and provide sentence stems for each section to help these students express their thoughts. Remind them to focus on content rather than grammar and mechanics. Challenge gifted students to research the concepts being discussed in class and share further research information in their journals. Allow students reading and writing below grade level to complete the section they are most comfortable with first to build their confidence. Guide a small group to complete the remainder of the sections.

Journal-Writing Strategies
for Social Studies *(cont.)*

Three-Part Journal *(cont.)*

Grades 1–2 Example

Part 1: What new information did you learn? What was your favorite part?
I learned that some fossils are not bones. They are bones that turned into rocks. A paleontologist is a scientist who studies fossils.
Part 2: What did you already know? How does the new information fit in with the old?
I knew that fossils are made in the ground. I knew that people dig carefully to take out the fossils. Sometimes the fossils are put into a museum. Now I know what kinds of tools they use when they dig.
Part 3: How can you use this information in your own life?
When I go to the dinosaur museum, I will know how they got from the ground to the museum. It takes a lot of hard work and patience!

Grades 3–5 Example

Part 1: What new information did you learn? What was your favorite part?
I learned that the city of Anaheim used to be a huge orchard. It was full of orange trees.
Part 2: What did you already know? How does the new information fit in with the old?
I knew that the area was developed in the 1950s, when Walt Disney started building Disneyland. I didn't realize how Disneyland helped make the city grow. I thought there were already lots of buildings and houses here.
Part 3: How can you use this information in your own life?
Now I understand how important Disneyland is to our community. I can't imagine what our city would be like if Disneyland had not been built here. Maybe a lot of our area would still be orchards filled with trees!

Journal-Writing Strategies for Social Studies (cont.)

Three-Part Journal (cont.)

Grades 6–8 Example

Part 1: What new information did you learn? What was your favorite part?
I learned about Queen Hatshepsut in Egypt. It is amazing that a woman ruled so large a kingdom that long ago. My favorite part was learning about how she tried to make her appearance more like a man, by wearing the short skirt of a man.

Part 2: What did you already know? How does the new information fit in with the old?
I had heard of Ramses the Great. I didn't know that there was also Ramses II and Ramses III. Now I understand how Ramses and Hatshepsut were connected.

Part 3: How can you use this information in your own life?
Using what I learned today, I am reminded that there are a great number of contributions that women have made in history. Sometimes we don't always hear about them. History is filled with the accomplishments of men, and I was very proud to learn about the life of Hatshepsut. She was ahead of her time. It shows me that my goal of becoming the first woman president of the United States is not impossible.

Name: _____

Three-Part Journal

Part 1: What new information did you learn? What was your favorite part?

Part 2: What did you already know? How does the new information fit in with the old?

Part 3: How can you use this information in your own life?

Taking Notes in Social Studies

Note-taking is a crucial skill for students in upper elementary grades and beyond. High school and college students do a significant amount of note-taking during classes and while reading, so it makes sense for this skill to be taught to our younger students. Teachers often ask students to take notes, or copy modeled notes, during a lecture. Some ask for notes as evidence of completing assigned independent reading. Additionally, notes can be useful as a review tool before an assessment.

Note-taking is also an important research skill, as it provides a system for organizing information. As students read various research sources, they must extract the larger overarching ideas and the supporting details. If students are to apply this information in a meaningful way, they must arrange the information in such a way that makes sense. Otherwise, the notes are simply a laundry list of random information. By providing instruction on effective note-taking systems, teachers can help their students become more efficient researchers.

It is important to note that this skill needs to be taught, with a clear explanation, teacher modeling, guided practice, and explicit feedback. As with any other strategy, students must reach a level of proficiency before they are expected to use the strategy independently. Teachers can employ the same instructional strategies that are effective when teaching other skills: make a transparency of the selection, conduct a think-aloud as the main ideas and details are identified, model how to use the designated note-taking strategy on the overhead or chart paper, and ask for student assistance to complete the notes. Upper elementary students may need the notes scaffolded for them, with some of the information filled in, in order to develop a useful set of notes.

Teachers can make explicit the connection between reading and writing by discussing how text structures are mirrored between the two. Students who are familiar with various text structures will be better able to learn and use the notes strategies. Informational text that is organized by main ideas will lend themselves well to a strategy such as a T-List, where main ideas are listed in one column and the corresponding details are listed in the other. Additionally, text that describes a series of concepts may be better suited to the Note-Taking System for Learning, where each concept has a section within the outline. Teachers may want to introduce one of these strategies immediately following a reading lesson on main idea and details. In this way, teachers can provide an authentic opportunity for students to apply that "reading" skill to a "writing" strategy.

To extend the value of note-taking, teachers can show students how to use their notes to apply new knowledge to a writing activity. Well organized notes are an excellent foundation for a well written assignment. Teachers can remind students to make use of their notes to begin a piece of writing, as they serve as an effective prewriting strategy. Again, this can show students the connection between reading and writing.

Note-Taking Strategies for Social Studies

Cornell Note-Taking System

Background Information

The Cornell Note-Taking System (Pauk 1988) strategy assists in teaching students about how to effectively take notes during a social studies lecture. This strategy teaches students to take clean notes and to organize the notes for the best study options later. It requires a lot of practice time for the students. Teach the Cornell Note-Taking System by providing modeling or practice each day and slowly incorporating the different stages of the system.

Grade Levels/Standards Addressed

Grades 3–5 (Standard 4.7)
Grades 6–8 (Standard 4.5)

Genres

Expository

Stages of Writing Process

Prewrite

Activity

Create or designate a notebook for the Cornell Note-Taking System sheets (page 101) so that sheets can be added or removed. Instruct students to write on only one side of the paper. The right side is the Notes column, for notes taken during the lecture. The left column of the page is the Recall column, where key words or phrases that summarize the notes are recorded. Before beginning a social studies lecture, explain that students should focus on the Notes column. Encourage them to use abbreviations or phrases and to write down the big ideas when taking notes. Students may need to skip lines to leave room for adding information later. Discuss the

notes that could be gleaned from the lecture and discuss the different ways that students can record this information. Remind students to focus on the main ideas and key terms of the content and to not get bogged down with too many details. After the lecture, instruct students to read through their notes and write down key points or terms in the Recall column. These key words or phrases will help them recall the main idea of each section of notes without having to read through the whole Notes section. Remind students to review their notes each day to place the information into long-term memory.

Variations

Have students use their notes to write questions about the material that might be asked on future tests. Or, instruct students to cover up the Notes side and use the cue words on the Recall side to describe the details of each concept. Students can verify what they have recited by uncovering the notes column and checking their work.

Differentiation

When working with ELLs, scaffold the Notes page by providing some of the main ideas to provide a preview of the information and shape their focus for the lecture. Challenge gifted students to add diagrams, maps, and charts in the notes column to visually portray processes or important concepts. For students who are reading and writing below grade level, preview the main ideas of the lecture and explain how to identify important as well as extraneous information. This discussion will help these students organize and understand their notes, and it will help cement information taught during the lecture.

Note-Taking Strategies for Social Studies (cont.)

Cornell Note-Taking System (cont.)

Grades 3–5 Example

Topic: __The Road to Revolution__

Recall	Notes
Boston Tea Party	-The Boston Tea party took place because of the Tea Act of 1773.
	-The Tea Act was a plan by the British to try and get the colonists to buy tea again.
Americans and the Colonists clash	-The Tea Act lowered the price of British tea, but the Americans didn't want to buy the tea because they didn't want to pay more taxes to the British.
British ships pull into American ports	-The British ships came into port, but the Americans prevented them from docking.
	-In December, British ships docked in Boston Harbor. The Americans wanted them to leave, but they would not.
Colonists dressed as Indians and tossed the tea	-A group of men dressed up as Indians boarded the ship in the middle of the night. They threw hundreds of chests filled with tea into the ocean to protest. This became known as the Boston Tea Party.

Grades 6–8 Example

Topic: __The Civil War Begins__

Recall	Notes
July 1861—picnickers gather to watch battle	-In July of 1861, families gathered in Manassas Junction to enjoy a picnic and to watch the first battle of the Civil War.
	-Most people thought it would be the first and last battle of the Civil War.
Union Army tries to capture Richmond	-The Union Army wanted to capture Richmond, VA, which was the capital of the Confederate States of America.
Battle became serious, people flee.	-The cannons and gunfire could be heard in the distance. The picnickers realize this is serious and they flee.
	-The battle became more severe, and the sightseers as well as the Union soldiers filled up the road back to Washington.
	-This was just the beginning of the deadliest war in the Civil War.

Name: _____

Cornell Note-Taking System

Directions: During a lecture, take notes in the Notes column, using short phrases and abbreviations. After the lecture, review your notes and write the key points in the Recall column.

Topic: _____

Recall	Notes

Note-Taking Strategies for Social Studies (cont.)

Note-Taking System for Learning

Background Information

Students in the upper elementary and middle school grades are required to take notes on lectures and presentations. Often, students do not have experience with or the understanding of how to take notes, and the Note-Taking System for Learning (Palmatier 1973) helps students learn this valuable skill.

Grade Levels/Standards Addressed

Grades 3–5 (Standard 4.7)
Grades 6–8 (Standard 4.5)

Genres

Expository

Stages of Writing Process

Prewrite

Activity

Before introducing this strategy, distribute copies of the Note-Taking System for Learning sheets (page 104). The strategy has three main components:

1. Recording—During a lecture, have students write down the main ideas and supporting details in outline form. Instruct them to leave space between main ideas as needed for future notes and additions. Palmatier suggests writing only on the front of the pages to avoid confusion later. Model for students how to take notes; after reading a passage from a social studies text, take notes on a chart or transparency to show how to choose the key points. Give students plenty of practice taking notes before expecting them to do it independently.

2. Organizing—When students have completed their notes, have them number the pages and staple them in order. Next, have students read through their notes and add labels in the left margin that describe the gist of the notes. This allows time for students to review what they have written and helps them identify any confusion they may have about the content. Students may also add to their notes, incorporating information from the text, lecture, or additional research that clarifies existing information. Use the blank side of the paper for this.

3. Studying—Once students have organized all the information in one place, instruct them to use their notes to study. The labels and information in the left margin provide a summary and overview of their notes.

Differentiation

Scaffold notes for ELLs by providing them with the main points. Then have them focus on adding details during the note-taking process. They will still have the opportunity to summarize and label their notes in the left margin. Challenge gifted students to add to their notes by reading a newspaper article or other social studies text. Be sure the new materials are at a challenging reading level. For students reading and writing below grade level, clearly define main ideas and details and provide examples of completed notes pages. Prior to the lecture, provide them with the main ideas so that they can listen for and record the details.

Note-Taking Strategies for Social Studies (cont.)

Note-Taking System for Learning (cont.)

Grades 3–5 Example

Subject: Gettysburg

I. Location and People
   a. Pennsylvania
   b. General Robert E. Lee
   c. Abraham Lincoln

II. Turning Point in the Civil War
   a. Dedicate cemetery in honor of soldiers that died
   b. The South never invaded the North again after that battle

III. Gettysburg Address
   a. Two minutes long
   b. Became the most famous speech

Grades 6–8 Example

Subject: The Great Depression

I. Causes
   a. Crash of the Stock Market
   b. Unsold Goods
   c. Bank Failures

II. Effects
   a. Workers without jobs
   b. Farmers go broke – the Dust Bowl
   c. No safe money

III. Solutions—Franklin D. Roosevelt
   a. The New Deal
   b. CCC
   c. TVA
   d. Social Security Act

Name: _____

Note-Taking System for Learning

Directions: During a lecture, write down the main ideas and supporting details in outline form.

Subject: _____

I. _____

    a. _____

    b. _____

    c. _____

    d. _____

II. _____

    a. _____

    b. _____

    c. _____

    d. _____

III. _____

    a. _____

    b. _____

    c. _____

    d. _____

Note-Taking Strategies for Social Studies *(cont.)*

T-List

Background Information

The T-List strategy (Chamot and O'Malley 1994; Hamp-Lyons 1983) organizes information into main ideas and details. It is also an effective alternative to quizzes and short-answer tests for assessing student comprehension. This strategy can facilitate question-and-answer discussions and oral summaries. The T-List is a visual representation of information that students can use to write about a given topic.

Grade Levels/Standards Addressed

Grades 3–5 (Standard 4.7)
Grades 6–8 (Standard 4.5)

Genres

Expository

Stages of Writing Process

Prewrite

Activity

Distribute copies of the T-List (page 107) or have students create their own by drawing a large "T" on a blank piece of paper. On the left side of the T-List, students list main ideas or key concepts from the reading passage or lecture. On the right side of the T-List, students record the corresponding details that support the main ideas. Explain to students that they will organize the main ideas and details of a social studies text or lecture on the chart. As the lesson proceeds, guide students in identifying the main ideas (in only two or three words) and writing them in the left-hand column. Students should then write the corresponding details in their own words rather than copying them from the text.

Differentiation

Fill in portions of the T-List prior to giving it to ELLs, and have them identify supportive details as they read. Also, be sure to preteach any challenging vocabulary words they might encounter. Challenge gifted students with the T-List by assigning a chapter and have students create and fill in a T-List independently. Organize them in a small group to compare their T-Lists and justify their decisions. For students who are reading and writing below grade level, provide the main ideas for the left-hand column as a scaffold.

Note-Taking Strategies for Social Studies (cont.)

T-List (cont.)

Grades 3–5 Example

Directions: Write the main ideas gained from the reading in the left-hand column. Then add details that support each main idea in the column on the right.

Subject: **Major Battles of the Civil War**

Main Ideas	Details
Battle of Bull Run	July 21, 1861: Union troops are surprised with defeat
Battle of Antietam	Sept. 17, 1862: bloodiest day of the Civil War (24,000 soldiers died)
Battle of Gettysburg	1863: Pennsylvania, Robert E. Lee, general for the South invades the North
Battle of Vicksburg	July 4, 1863: North wins victory and captures Confederate stronghold of Vicksburg, Mississippi

Grades 6–8 Example

Directions: Write the main ideas gained from the reading in the left-hand column. Then add details that support each main idea in the column on the right.

Subject: **Federal Government**

Main Ideas	Details
Judicial Branch	Supreme Court -interpret the laws -judges serve a life term -nominated by president
Executive Branch	President of the United States -can serve a maximum of two four-year terms -must have been born in the U.S. -must be elected by the people
Legislative Branch	-create and pass laws for the country House of Representatives -serve two-year terms Senate -serve six-year terms

Name: _____

T–List

Directions: Write the main ideas gained from the reading in the left-hand column. Then add details that support each main idea in the column on the right.

Main Ideas	Details

Using Diagrams and Maps in Social Studies

The Reading-Writing Connection

Just as using diagrams and maps can help students identify the text structure to improve their reading comprehension, these tools can also improve students' writing abilities. Students must be able to recognize the patterns in a variety of writing genres in order to apply those same patterns to their own writing. Diagrams and maps are not only used for reading comprehension. They are also the key to effectively beginning a writing piece to plan and organize their information. Therefore, social studies teachers who are working toward developing the writing skills of their students can emphasize this with their students.

Text Structure

There are different elements to text structure worthy of examination. Instructional approaches range from highlighting external text features (i.e. illustrations, chapter headings, indices, etc.) to identifying sentence and paragraph organizational patterns (i.e. compare and contrast, description, etc.) to visually representing the organization of the ideas in the text through graphic organizers (i.e. Venn diagrams, concept maps, etc.).

The direct instruction of text structure is intended to help students anticipate, monitor, and comprehend what they are reading, in order to organize and communicate the information in writing. Using text structures helps students study model texts for their own writing pieces. If students know what the features are of each particular genre, they spend less time reworking a writing piece and more time effectively planning it in the early stages of writing. In addition, students who are familiar and comfortable with a wide variety of text structures can write with greater ease and can choose to write in the structure that best suits their needs.

Internal Text Structure

The internal text structure refers to how the words and paragraphs are put together. The purpose of information text is to tell, show, describe, or explain (Vacca and Vacca 2005). For the writer to communicate information easily, the information must be presented through the logical connections that exist between ideas. Text patterns have emerged in informational texts to aid in the expression of these logical connections. According to Vacca and Vacca (2005), there are five patterns of text that dominate informational writing: description, sequence, compare and contrast, cause and effect, and problem and solution. Each structure is represented in this section by a diagram or map that students can use to plan their writing.

Description—The information being presented about a topic (object, person, animal, idea, event) includes facts, characteristics, traits, and features.

Sequence—The facts, events, or concepts are presented in sequential order. The topic is developed in order of importance, or the sequence or steps in a process are given.

Compare and Contrast—The similarities (comparison) and differences (contrast) among facts, people, events, and concepts are presented.

Cause and Effect—The information is presented to make clear that certain things (effects) happen as a result of other things (causes).

Problem and Solution—The development of problem and possible solutions to it are presented.

Diagramming and Mapping Strategies for Social Studies

Frame

Background Information

Frames (Ryder and Graves 2003) are charts that organize important information in rows and columns to illustrate relationships between the main ideas and details. Frames assist students in distinguishing important concepts from less important details and help them to compare and contrast information. Different types of Frames can be used for different purposes (Ryder and Graves 2003). Matrix Frames are best used in social studies classes to compare and contrast information, examine cause-and-effect relationships, and analyze forms and functions. Frames help students write about nonfiction social studies topics by organizing and structuring information. When students write summaries based on the information in the Frame, it allows them to reflect on the content, elaborate on the application, and note relationships or draw distinctions between broader concepts and related information (Ryder and Graves 2003).

Grade Levels/Standards Addressed

Grades 3–5 (Standard 1.1, 4.7)
Grades 6–8 (Standard 1.1, 4.5)

Genres

Expository

Stages of Writing Process

Prewrite

Preparation

Consider how the main ideas from the selected text can be compared, what features they share, and what specific features or characteristics they possess (Ryder and Graves 2003). Draw the Frame (page 111) by creating and labeling the columns and rows. Write the main topics, ideas, and concepts in the rows and list the categories for the characteristics and/or relationships in the columns.

Activity

Tell students they will use a graphic organizer called a Frame to organize the key information in a selection of text. Remind them that good writers need to gather information before writing, and it helps to keep this information as organized as possible. Distribute copies of the prepared Frame with the rows and columns labeled. Allow time for students to review it and predict what information might fit within it. After reading the selected text, discuss the content and have students fill in the boxes in each row and column as a class or in small groups. Encourage students to add their prior knowledge to the Matrix Frame as well. Students can use the information to assist them in writing a summary or a report on the assigned topic.

Differentiation

Discuss any unfamiliar words and information with ELLs before beginning the lesson to assist them in completing the Frame. Challenge gifted students to complete the Frame independently, including determining the column and row titles. In addition, have them create a new Frame with a different text passage and compare the two. Give students reading and writing below grade level a Frame that is partially completed to assist them.

Diagramming and Mapping Strategies for Social Studies (cont.)

Frame (cont.)

Grades 3–5 Example

Topic: **Famous Women in American History**

Famous Woman	Accomplishments	Time Period
Sacagawea	interpreter for Lewis & Clark	1800s
Dolly Madison	First Lady, saved important documents when British stormed the White House	early 1800s
Clara Barton	dedicated nurse during the Civil War	1800s
Elizabeth Cady Stanton	fought for women's rights	1848
Dorothea Pix	led a movement to improve the care of the mentally ill	1800s

Grades 6–8 Example

Topic: **Bill of Rights – Freedoms**

Order	Freedom	Description
1st	religion	freedom to worship according to beliefs
2nd	the press	right to publish newspapers, magazines, and books
3rd	speech	right of people to say what they believe
4th	assembly	right of people to gather and act together for political action
5th	petition	right of people to ask government to change a law

Frame

Directions: Write in the topic for the Frame and the titles for each column. Then fill in each box with information from the text.

Topic: _____

Diagramming and Mapping Strategies for Social Studies *(cont.)*

Venn Diagram

Background Information

The Venn Diagram (Venn 1880) compares and contrasts two items, terms, or concepts. In the social studies classroom, the Venn Diagram is especially useful in helping students articulate and write about what they are learning in a manner that visually illustrates similarities and differences. Using the Venn Diagram also requires students to write descriptions in their own words and to condense and summarize their statements. It is also a useful prewriting strategy because it organizes the information, so students can begin writing an effective draft.

Grade Levels/Standards Addressed

Grades 1–2 (Standard 1.1, 4.2)
Grades 3–5 (Standard 1.1, 4.7)
Grades 6–8 (Standard 1.1, 4.5)

Genres

Expository

Stages of Writing Process

Prewrite

Activity

Select two social studies concepts to compare and contrast. Begin by telling students that they will organize information using a graphic organizer called a Venn Diagram to compare and contrast two topics or concepts. Distribute copies of the Venn Diagram (page 115) and emphasize that similarities are listed in the center and differences are listed in the outer sections of the circles. Have students write the concepts at the top of each circle and discuss these two concepts to activate prior knowledge about their similarities and differences.

As students read the selected text, instruct them to look for information to include on their diagrams. List the unique characteristics and attributes of each concept in the appropriate outer sections and the commonalities in the center section.

Differentiation

Scaffold the Venn Diagram for ELLs by listing some of the characteristics. Provide a few examples to get them started and to clarify what you are looking for in this assignment. Instruct gifted students to complete the Venn Diagram without any discussion or support from the text. Have those students verify their characteristics and attributes with reading after they have completed the Venn Diagram. When finished, gifted students can then write a compare/contrast essay using the notes they recorded on the Venn Diagram. Allow students who read and write below grade level to work with a partner or small group.

Diagramming and Mapping Strategies for Social Studies *(cont.)*

Venn Diagram *(cont.)*

Grades 1–2 Example

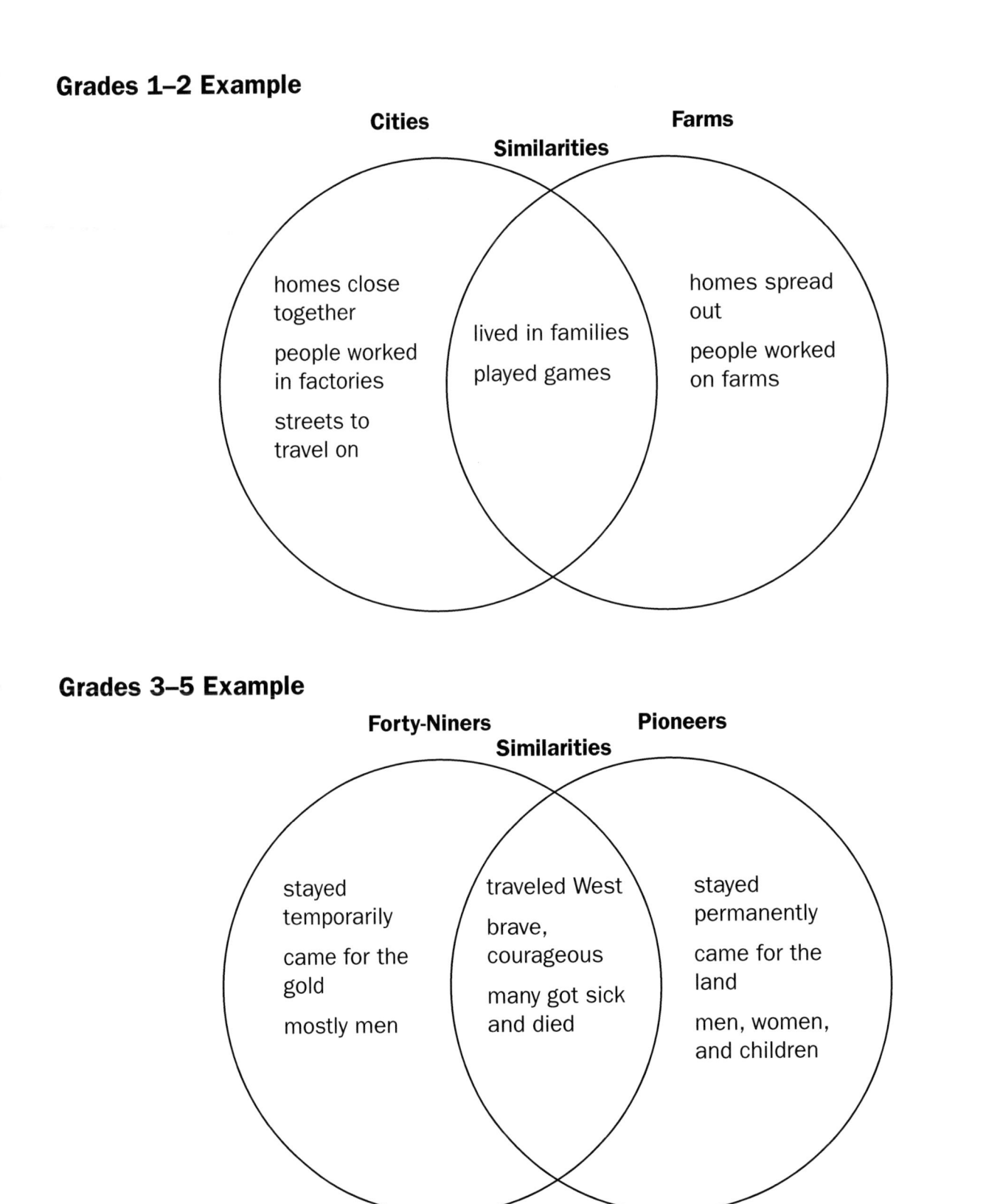

Cities

Farms

Similarities

homes close together

people worked in factories

streets to travel on

lived in families

played games

homes spread out

people worked on farms

Grades 3–5 Example

Forty-Niners

Pioneers

Similarities

stayed temporarily

came for the gold

mostly men

traveled West

brave, courageous

many got sick and died

stayed permanently

came for the land

men, women, and children

Diagramming and Mapping Strategies
for Social Studies *(cont.)*
Venn Diagram *(cont.)*

Grades 6–8 Example

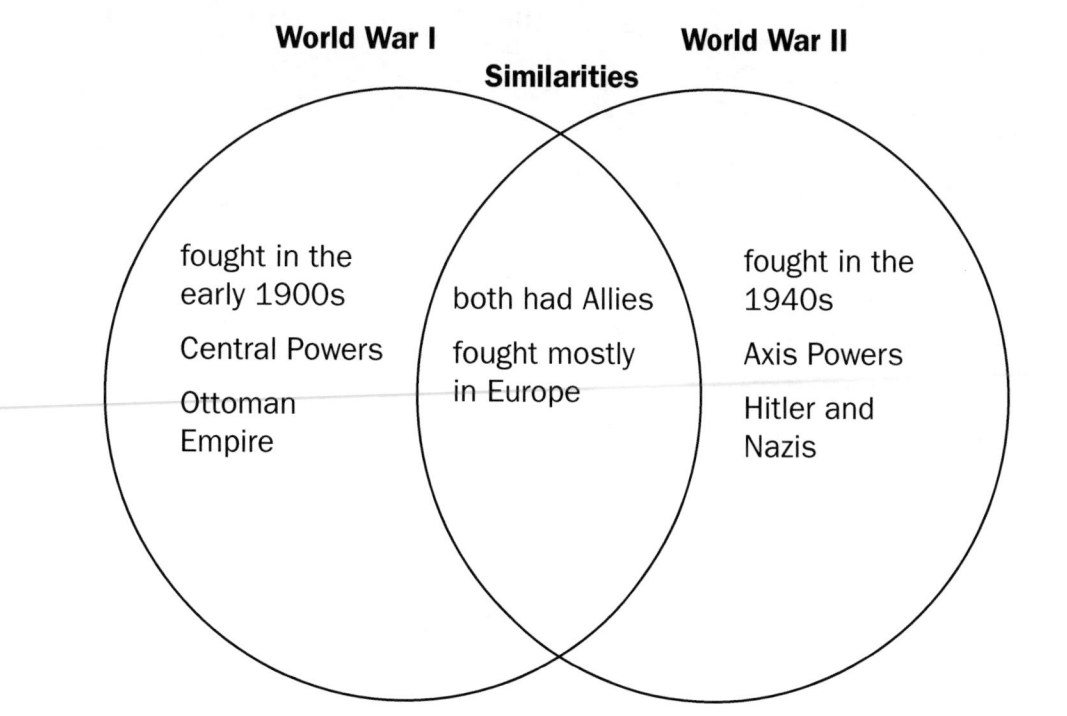

#50058—Writing Strategies for Social Studies   © *Shell Education*

Venn Diagram

Directions: Write on the top two lines the concepts you are comparing and contrasting. List the ways in which they are similar in the center section of the Venn Diagram. Write the ways they are unique in the outer sections of the circles.

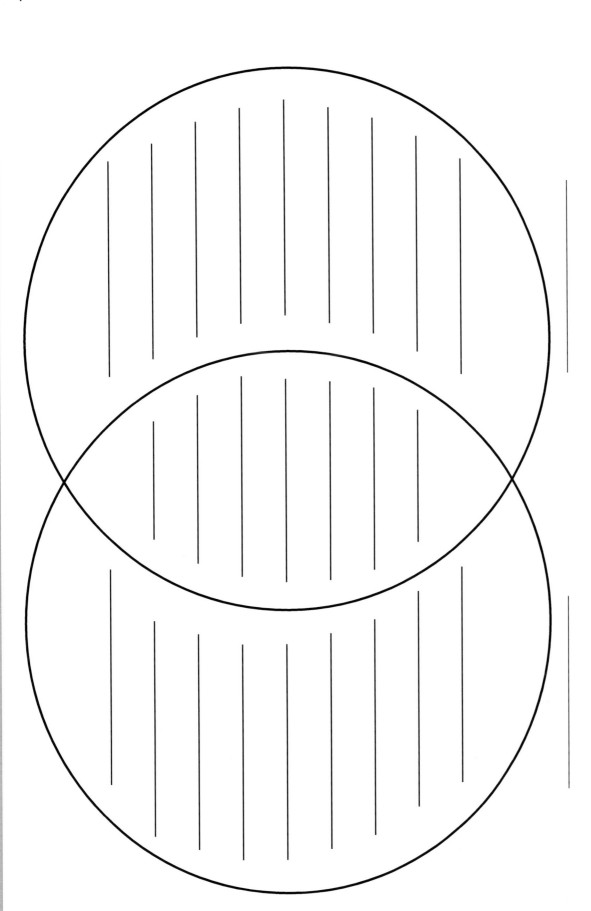

Diagramming and Mapping Strategies for Social Studies *(cont.)*

Triangular Venn Diagram

Background Information

Use the Triangular Venn Diagram to compare three topics or concepts. It not only compares the items but also shows the interconnectedness among all three topics or concepts. When introducing this strategy, use basic concepts that are easy to understand, so students can learn the procedure. Remind students that the purpose of using a graphic organizer is to arrange the information in a way that makes sense, so it can be useful later for writing activities or projects.

Grade Levels/Standards Addressed

Grades 3–5 (Standard 1.1, 4.7)
Grades 6–8 (Standard 1.1, 4.5)

Genres

Expository

Stages of Writing Process

Prewrite

Activity

Determine the three concepts to discuss and compare. Distribute copies of the Triangular Venn Diagram (page 118) and label each of the large shaded triangles with the three concepts to compare. Discuss as a class the attributes of each concept:

- **How are these three concepts unique?** Write characteristics under each heading. These notes should give a brief summary or overview of each concept stating how each concept is unique and different from the others.

- **How is each pair of concepts similar to one another?** Compare each concept individually with another concept and discuss the characteristics that they share. Record this information inside the small white triangles in between the shaded triangles.

- **How are these three concepts interconnected?** Record information that all three concepts share in the center shaded triangle. This information must be valid for all three concepts.

On the back of the Triangular Venn Diagram, have students record information that they learned from this process. What insights did they gain? How will this new information change the way they think about these concepts? Discuss student findings as a class.

Differentiation

ELLs will need scaffolding on the Triangular Venn Diagram. Fill in portions of the characteristics for each concept. Encourage gifted students to complete this activity independently, then model for other students how to complete the diagram and how to determine which characteristics are important and which are extraneous information. Provide small-group instruction and preteaching of the diagram for students who are reading and writing below grade level.

Diagramming and Mapping Strategies
for Social Studies *(cont.)*

Triangular Venn Diagram *(cont.)*

Grades 3–8 Example

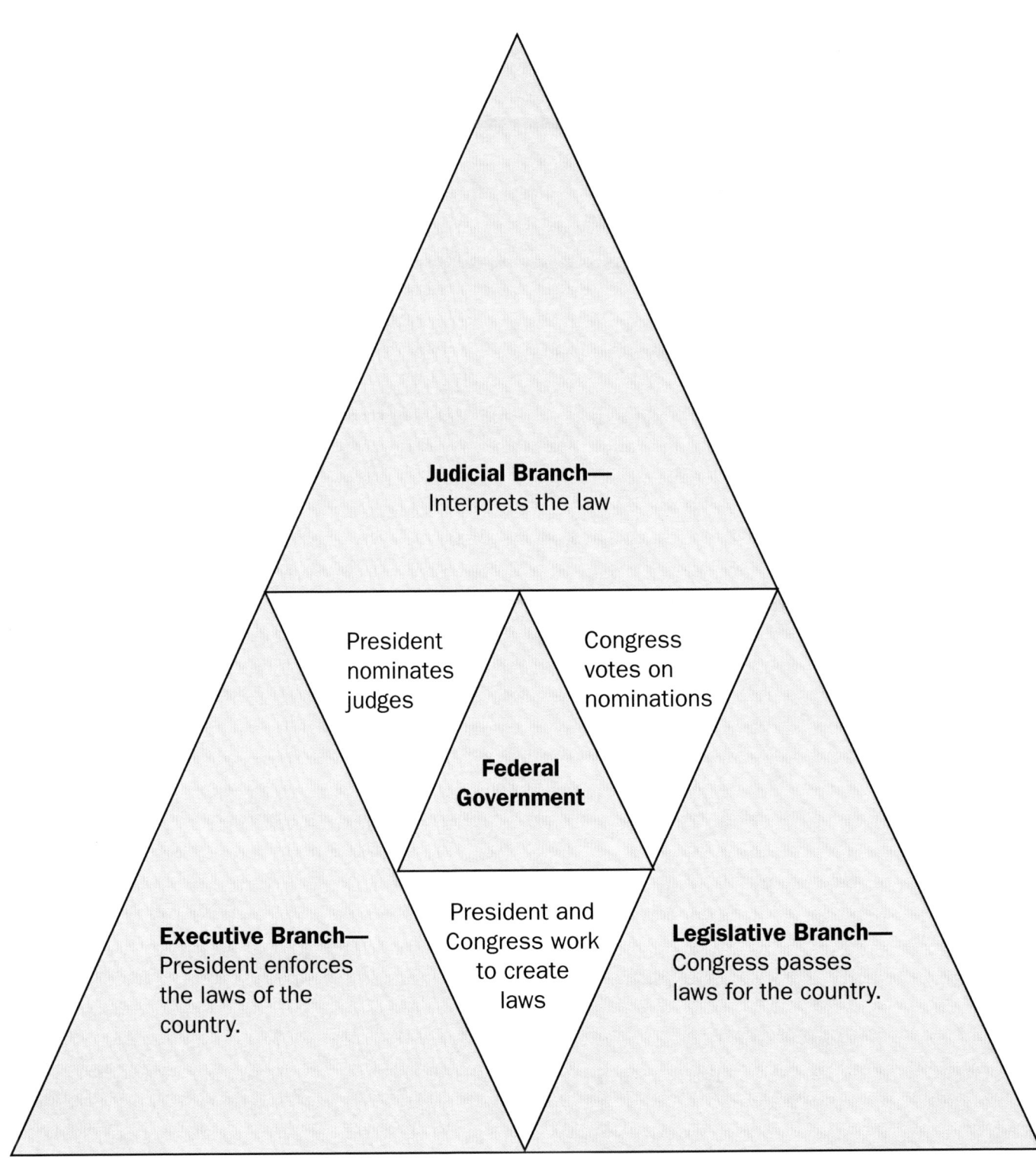

Name: _____

Triangular Venn Diagram

Directions: Use this diagram to compare and contrast three topics or concepts. In the outer triangles, write the unique features of each topic or concept. In the three interior triangles, record how each pair of concepts are similar. In the center triangle, write down what all three topics have in common.

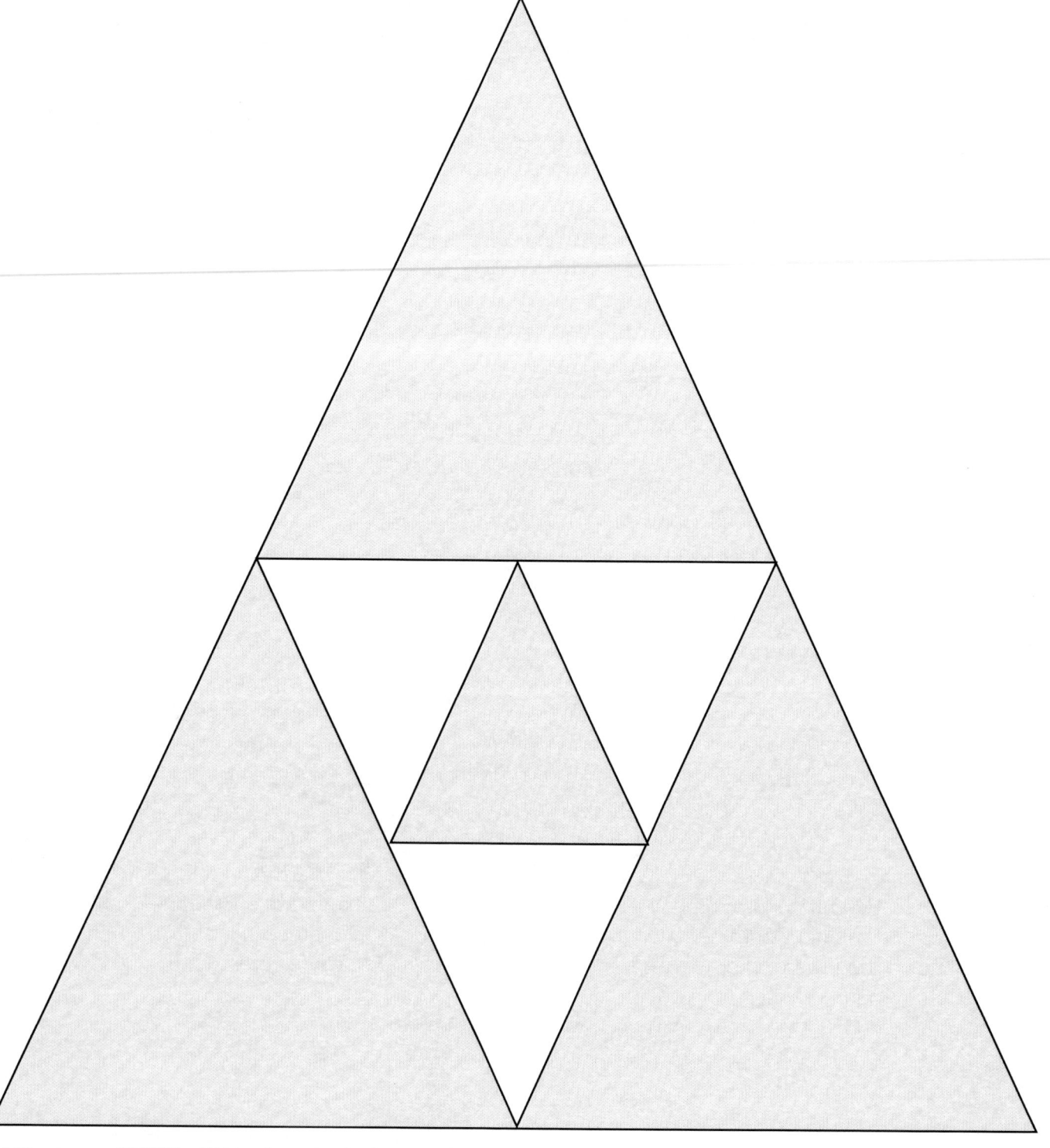

#50058—*Writing Strategies for Social Studies*   © *Shell Education*

Diagramming and Mapping Strategies for Social Studies *(cont.)*

Cause-and-Effect Map

Background Information

A Cause-and-Effect Map is a graphic organizer that helps organize information about the causes or effects of an event, a crucial skill needed for studying social studies. The Cause-and-Effect Map encourages students to use higher-order thinking skills that are key to understanding social studies concepts. Students can then use the Cause-and-Effect Map to organize information for different scientific writing projects.

Grade Levels/Standards Addressed

Grades 1–2 (Standard 1.1, 4.2)
Grades 3–5 (Standard 1.1, 4.7)
Grades 6–8 (Standard 1.1, 4.5)

Genres

Expository

Stages of Writing Process

Prewrite

Activity

Prior to reading about a specific social studies topic or completing a social studies experiment, explain that students will analyze causes and effects throughout the course of this activity. If needed, share several examples of a cause-and-effect relationship, especially in the primary grades. Distribute copies of the Cause-and-Effect Map (page 122) for students to complete and make sure they understand how to use it. Depending on the nature of the social studies text or the experiment, focus on either the cause(s) or effect(s) first.

- Ask questions that can help identify the cause(s): *What happens or changes the situation? Where does everything begin? What produces the effect?* Once students have identified the cause, they write a description of it. The more descriptive they are, the better they will be able to identify the effects.

- Ask questions that can help students identify the effect(s): *What is the result of the cause? What happened after the cause or the change? What happened next?* Make sure that students identify all the effects, if there are more than one. Encourage them to think about any effects that may not be obvious.

Differentiation

Model how to complete the Cause-and-Effect Map and provide examples for ELLs. Encourage discussion first, then allow them to work in pairs to complete the Cause-and-Effect Map. They can also use pictures. Encourage gifted students to use higher-level thinking skills: Have them alter the causes and predict how the effects would be different based on those causes. Use prompting and questioning with students reading and writing below grade level to help them identify the more complex effects or results. Or, provide the information for one side of the map and ask them to complete the other side.

Diagramming and Mapping Strategies
for Social Studies *(cont.)*

Cause-and-Effect Map *(cont.)*

Grades 1–2 Example

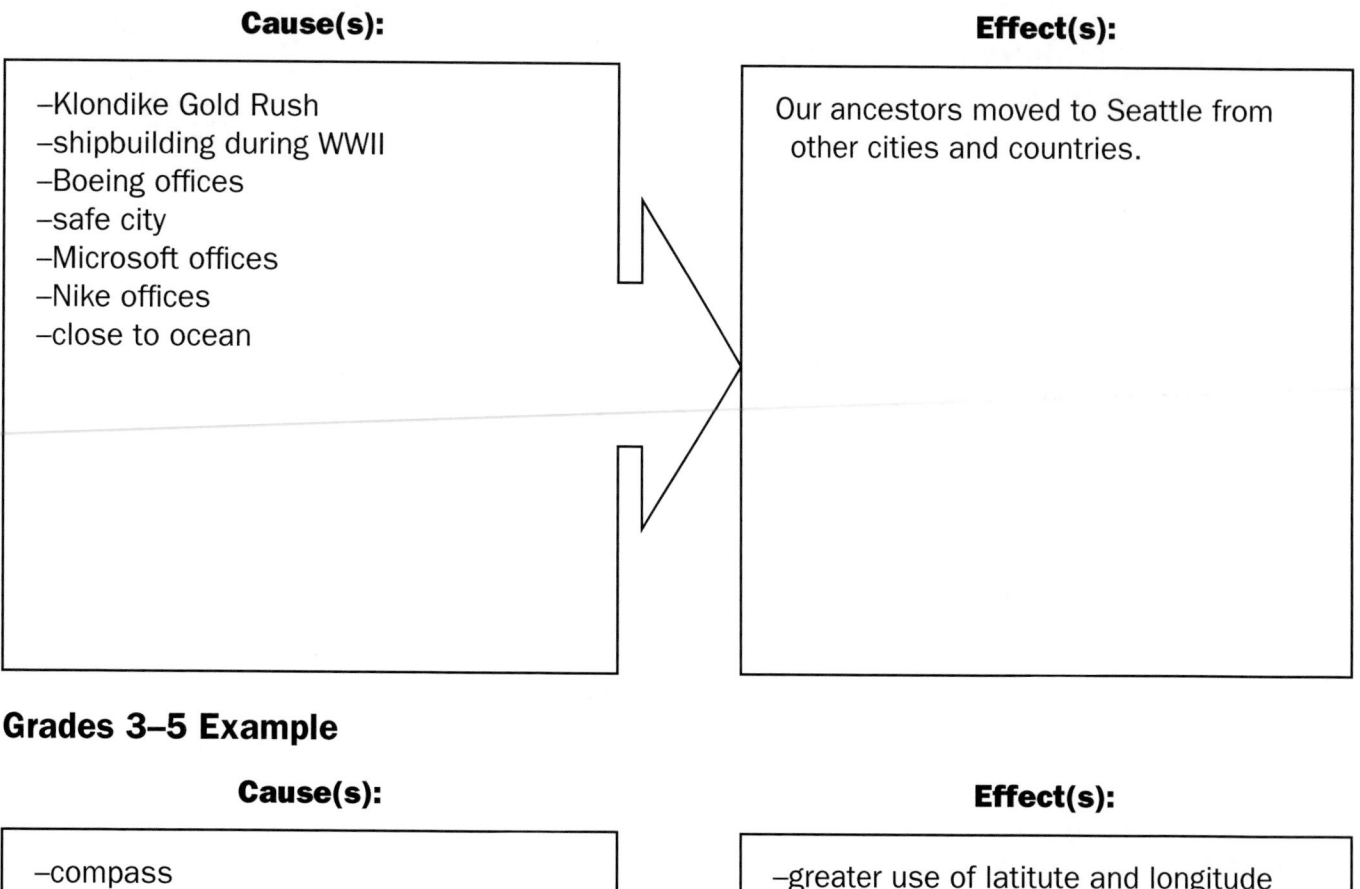

Cause(s):

- –Klondike Gold Rush
- –shipbuilding during WWII
- –Boeing offices
- –safe city
- –Microsoft offices
- –Nike offices
- –close to ocean

Effect(s):

Our ancestors moved to Seattle from other cities and countries.

Grades 3–5 Example

Cause(s):

- –compass
- –sextant
- –astrolabe
- –chronometer

Effect(s):

- –greater use of latitute and longitude for navigating the oceans and seas

- –increased exploration of North America by European explorers

Diagramming and Mapping Strategies
for Social Studies *(cont.)*

Cause-and-Effect Map *(cont.)*

Grades 6–8 Example

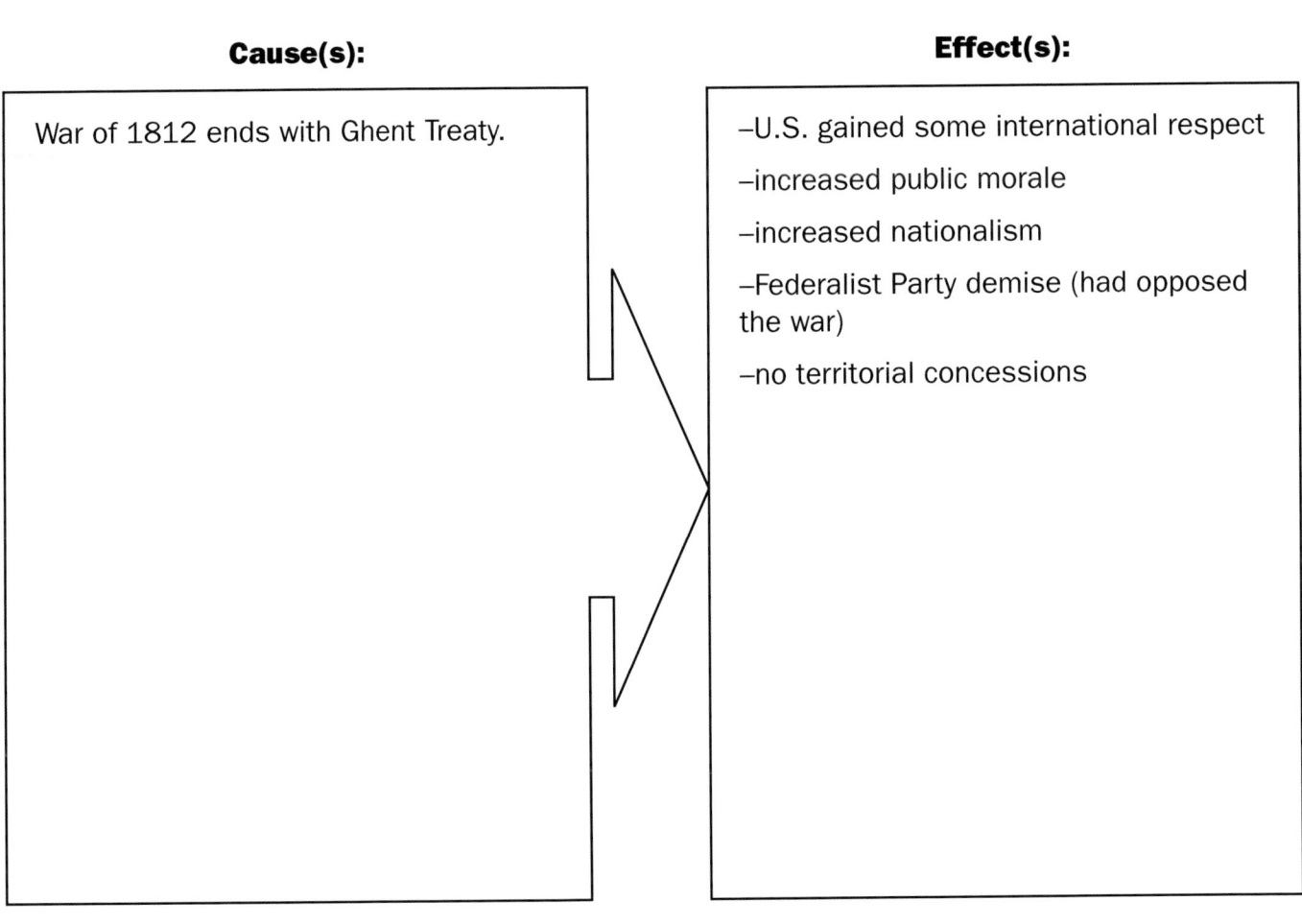

Cause(s):

War of 1812 ends with Ghent Treaty.

Effect(s):

–U.S. gained some international respect

–increased public morale

–increased nationalism

–Federalist Party demise (had opposed the war)

–no territorial concessions

Name: _____

Cause-and-Effect Map

Directions: Complete the graphic organizer by writing the causes and effects.

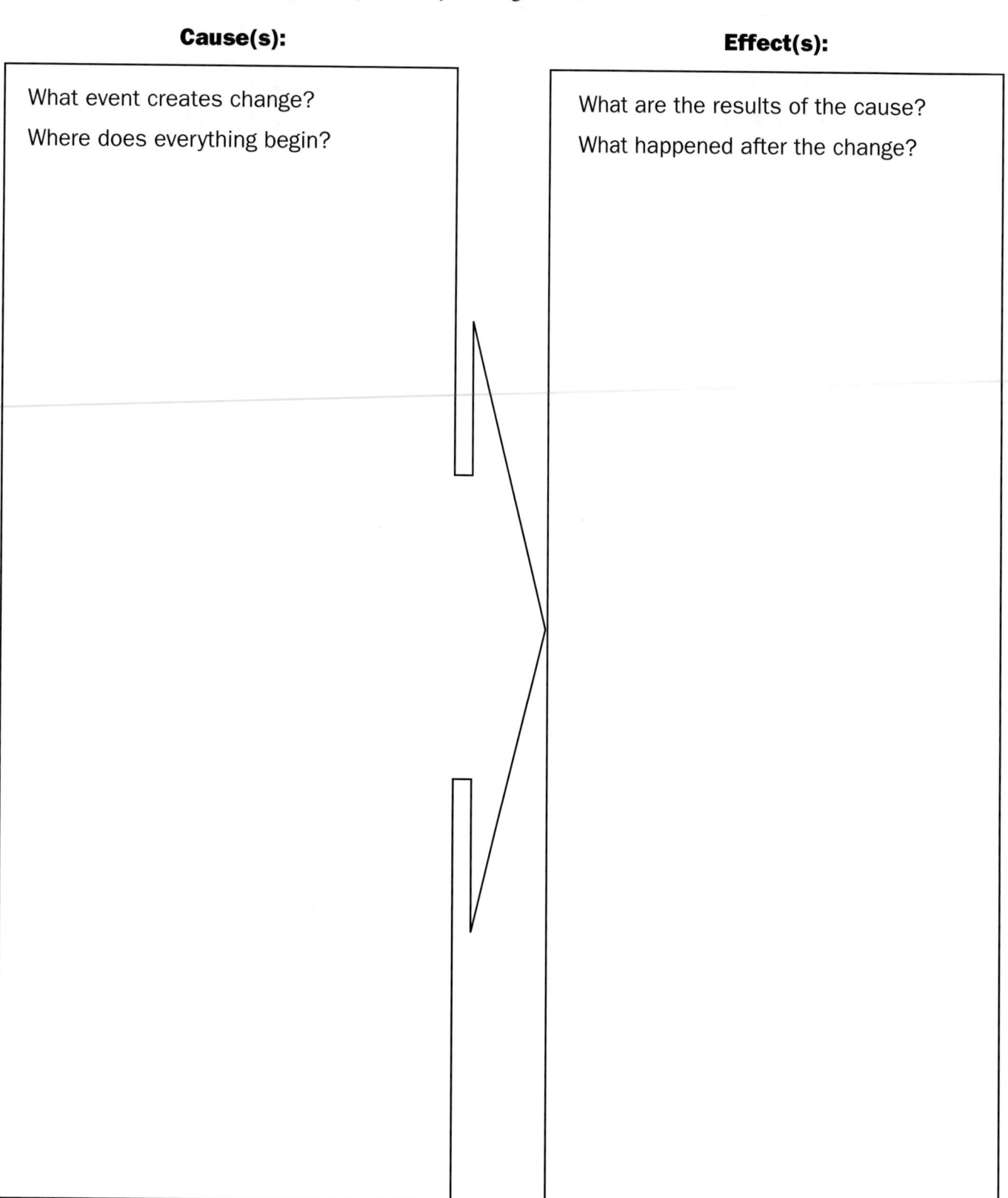

Cause(s):	Effect(s):
What event creates change? Where does everything begin?	What are the results of the cause? What happened after the change?

#50058—Writing Strategies for Social Studies © *Shell Education*

Diagramming and Mapping Strategies for Social Studies (cont.)

Semantic Word Map

Background Information

Semantic Word Maps (Heimlich and Pittelman 1986 as cited by Ryder and Graves 2003) allow students to clarify the meaning of concepts and identify connections to other related words by creating a map. This strategy is appropriate for studying a specific concept that has multiple vocabulary words. According to Nagy and Scott (2000), mapping the interconnectedness of social studies vocabulary words is a way for students to organize and store information in the brain. Because this strategy builds a bridge between new information and previous knowledge and prior experiences, it also can be used as a pre-assessment to see what students already know about a given topic. Students can add to their Semantic Word Maps after they have completed the reading. Students also can use the maps to help them review information at the end of a unit of study or to write a paragraph or essay.

Grade Levels/Standards Addressed

Grades 1–2 (Standard 1.1, 4.2)
Grades 3–5 (Standard 1.1, 4.7)
Grades 6–8 (Standard 1.1, 4.5)

Genres

Expository

Stages of Writing Process

Prewrite

Activity

Determine the central concept of the assigned reading passage. After introducing the concept, lead a brainstorming session to create a list of words about it. Record all student ideas on the board or a transparency. Encourage students to explain how these words relate to bigger ideas, events, characteristics, and examples, and help them move from the words to the concepts. Once the bigger categories have been determined, have the students organize the words into categories. By doing this, students create a Semantic Word Map (page 126) that shows big ideas, small ideas, and how all the ideas interconnect. Instruct students to share and explain their maps in a small group, making sure to justify and explain their reasons for choosing each word for each category.

Differentiation

Allow ELLs to work in small groups on this activity, so they can hear how other students determine categories and fit words into these categories. Encourage gifted students to incorporate additional or more complex words and categories, using resources to help them determine appropriate placement. Students reading and writing below grade level should work independently to generate a list of words and then work with a partner to determine the categories and the placement of the words. Working with partners provides students with support. Do not place these students in groups for this activity as they will "fall through the cracks."

Diagramming and Mapping Strategies
for Social Studies (cont.)

Semantic Word Map (cont.)

Grades 1–2 Example

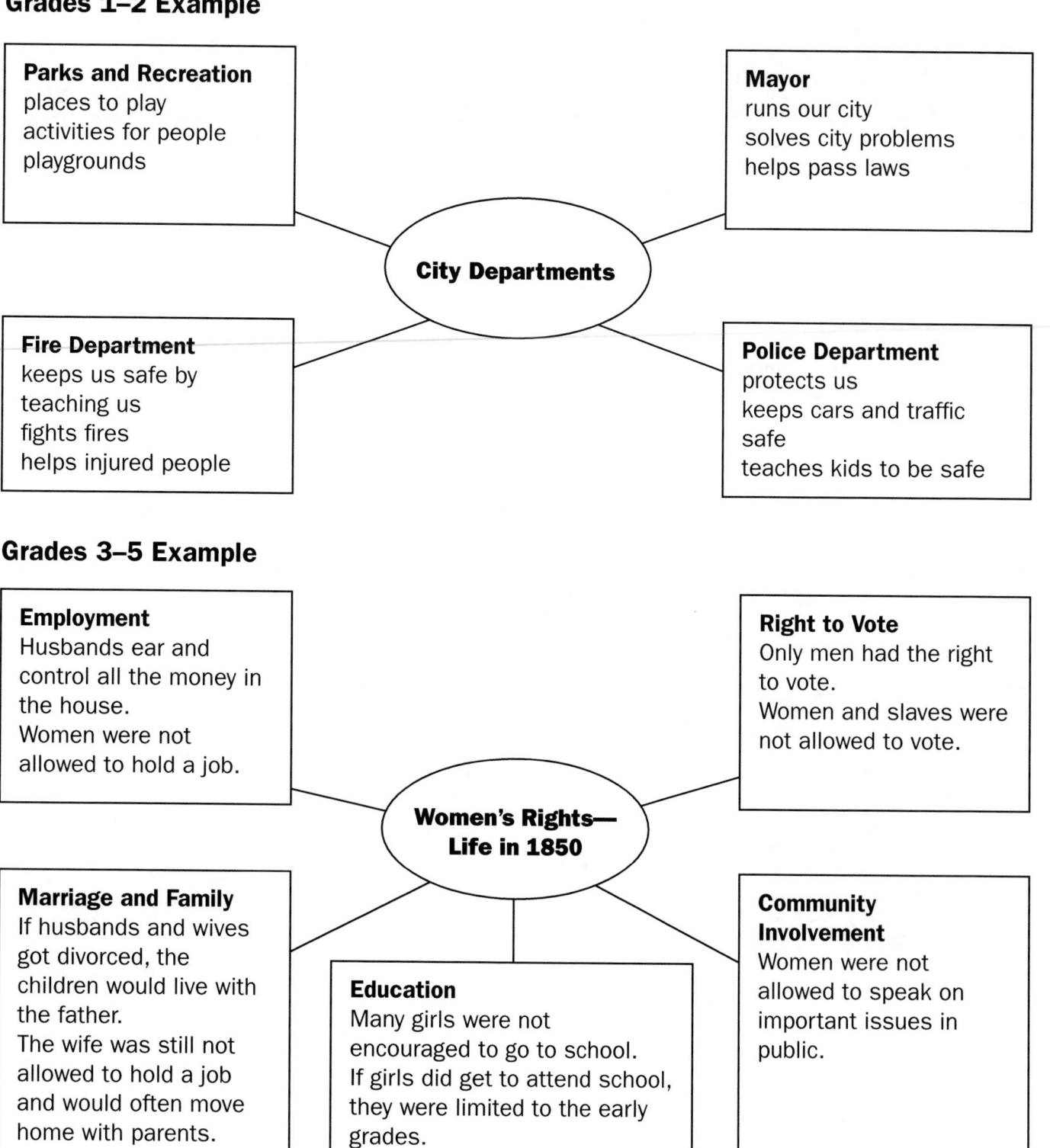

Parks and Recreation
places to play
activities for people
playgrounds

Mayor
runs our city
solves city problems
helps pass laws

City Departments

Fire Department
keeps us safe by
teaching us
fights fires
helps injured people

Police Department
protects us
keeps cars and traffic
safe
teaches kids to be safe

Grades 3–5 Example

Employment
Husbands ear and
control all the money in
the house.
Women were not
allowed to hold a job.

Right to Vote
Only men had the right
to vote.
Women and slaves were
not allowed to vote.

**Women's Rights—
Life in 1850**

Marriage and Family
If husbands and wives
got divorced, the
children would live with
the father.
The wife was still not
allowed to hold a job
and would often move
home with parents.

Education
Many girls were not
encouraged to go to school.
If girls did get to attend school,
they were limited to the early
grades.

**Community
Involvement**
Women were not
allowed to speak on
important issues in
public.

Diagramming and Mapping Strategies
for Social Studies *(cont.)*

Semantic Word Map *(cont.)*

Grades 6–8 Example

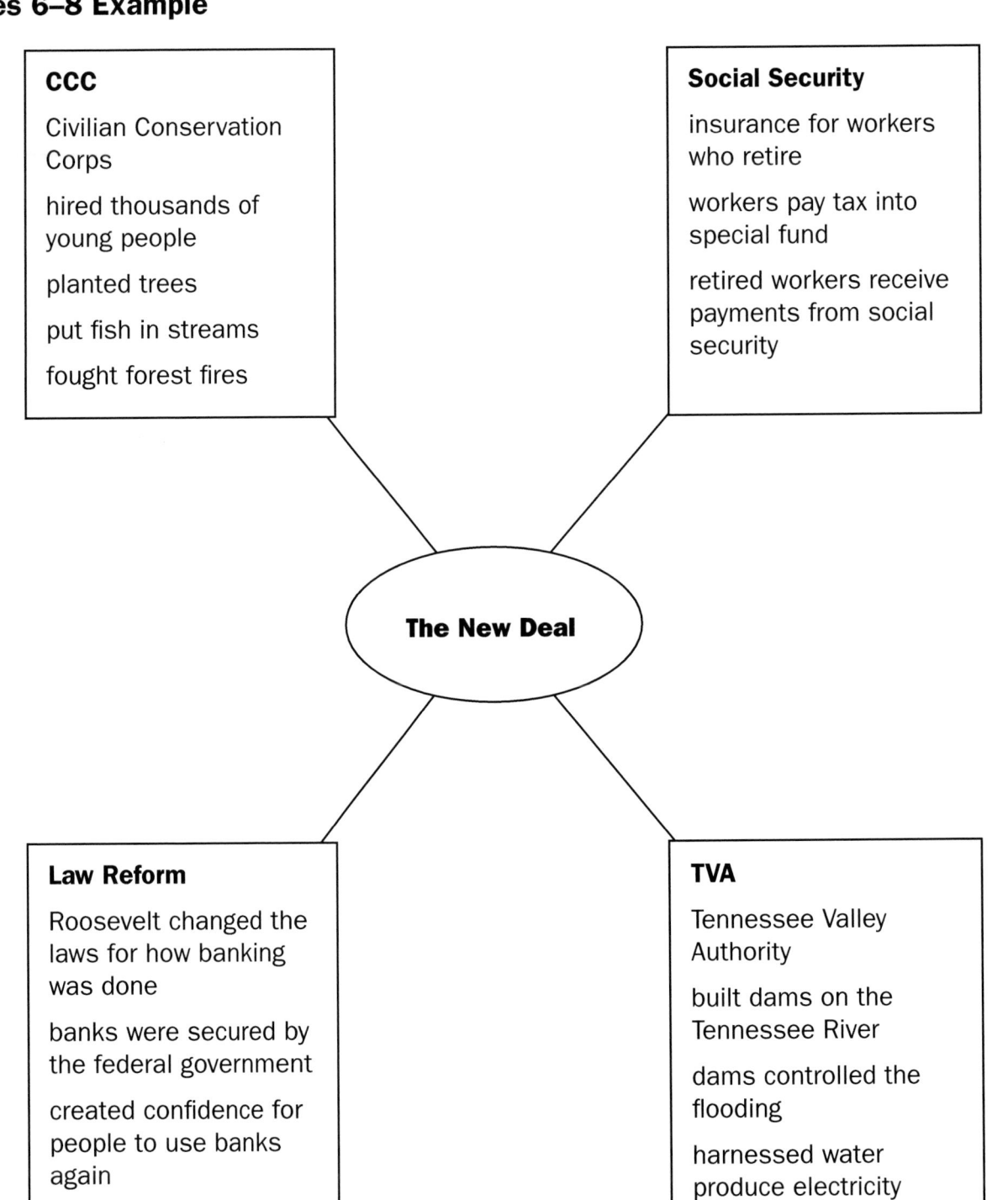

CCC

Civilian Conservation Corps

hired thousands of young people

planted trees

put fish in streams

fought forest fires

Social Security

insurance for workers who retire

workers pay tax into special fund

retired workers receive payments from social security

The New Deal

Law Reform

Roosevelt changed the laws for how banking was done

banks were secured by the federal government

created confidence for people to use banks again

TVA

Tennessee Valley Authority

built dams on the Tennessee River

dams controlled the flooding

harnessed water produce electricity

Name: _____

Semantic Word Map

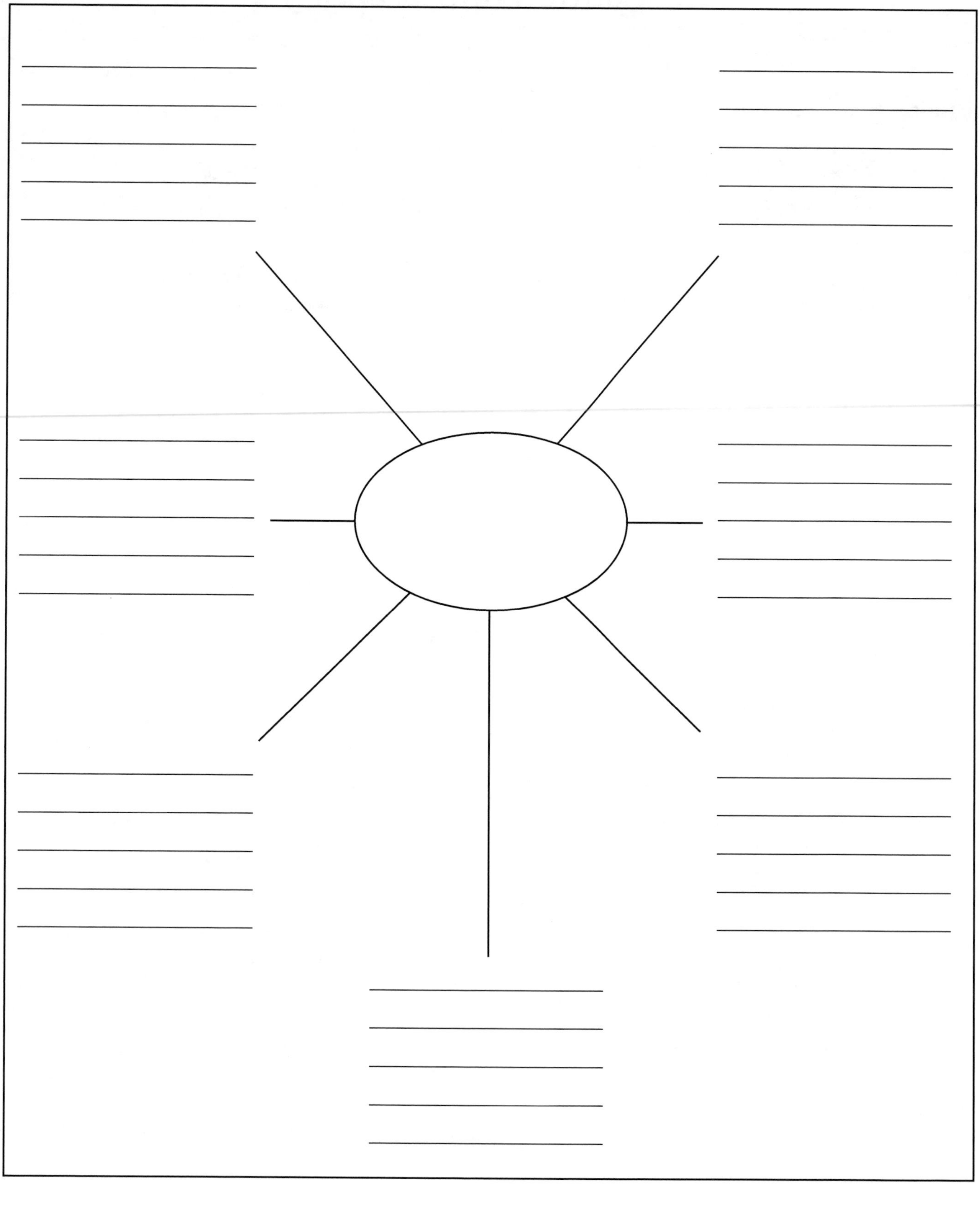

#50058—*Writing Strategies for Social Studies*   © *Shell Education*

Diagramming and Mapping Strategies for Social Studies *(cont.)*

Concept Map

Background Information

The Concept Map graphic organizer displays a visual representation of concepts and their relationships discussed in social studies texts (West, Farmer, and Wolff 1991). A Concept Map is generally organized in a hierarchical manner, moving from broad categories to specific categories. It resembles a flow chart in that the concepts are linked together with lines and arrows. This is an effective strategy to use prior to a social studies reading assignment; it prepares students for the material they will be reading and assists them in making connections between concepts. Following the reading, students can use their research skills to add or revise information. Concept Maps also help students organize information before they write. Each concept and its supporting details can then be logically and easily developed into a paragraph.

Grade Levels/Standards Addressed

Grades 3–5 (Standard 1.1, 4.7)
Grades 6–8 (Standard 1.1, 4.5)

Genres

Expository

Stages of Writing Process

Prewrite

Preparation

Read the assigned material and identify the most important concepts, as well as words and phrases related to these concepts. Then organize the concepts and identify the relationships and connections among them. Write a descriptive title that generates interest and increases curiosity.

Activity

Display the prepared Concept Map—outline only—on a chart or transparency. Distribute blank Concept Maps so students can write down their own information and learn to create the map independently. Write the title on the class map and have students predict what they think the reading passage will be about. Allow plenty of time for students to share, either in pairs or as a whole class, their background knowledge. Have students read the text, then meet again as a class to determine the most important concepts presented in the text. Write these on the Concept Map. Instruct students to identify and record on their maps details relating to each major concept. When finished, allow students to share their findings with a small group. Reassemble as a class and invite students to present the information they gathered. Incorporate their information into the class map. Use the presentation time to clarify misunderstandings and determine the level of knowledge students have developed about the topic.

Variation

Reverse the activity by making a list of all of the terms and categories that belong in a concept map. Distribute a blank concept map and have students place all the information in the correct spaces on the concept map. When finished, have students compare their maps with each other.

Diagramming and Mapping Strategies for Social Studies *(cont.)*

Concept Map *(cont.)*

Differentiation

Scaffold the map for ELLs and students reading below grade level by providing some of the concepts to help guide them as they fill out the map. Use specific shapes and colors on the map to create a more visual connection for these students. If desired, pair these students with partners to complete the Concept Maps. Challenge gifted students to read an additional piece of text and add to their maps.

Extension

Use the Concept Map as a guide for further reading on the topics presented or as an outline for writing social studies assignments. Encourage students to continue to add information, highlight key points, and use the map for review.

Diagramming and Mapping Strategies for Social Studies (cont.)

Concept Map (cont.)

Grades 3–5 Example

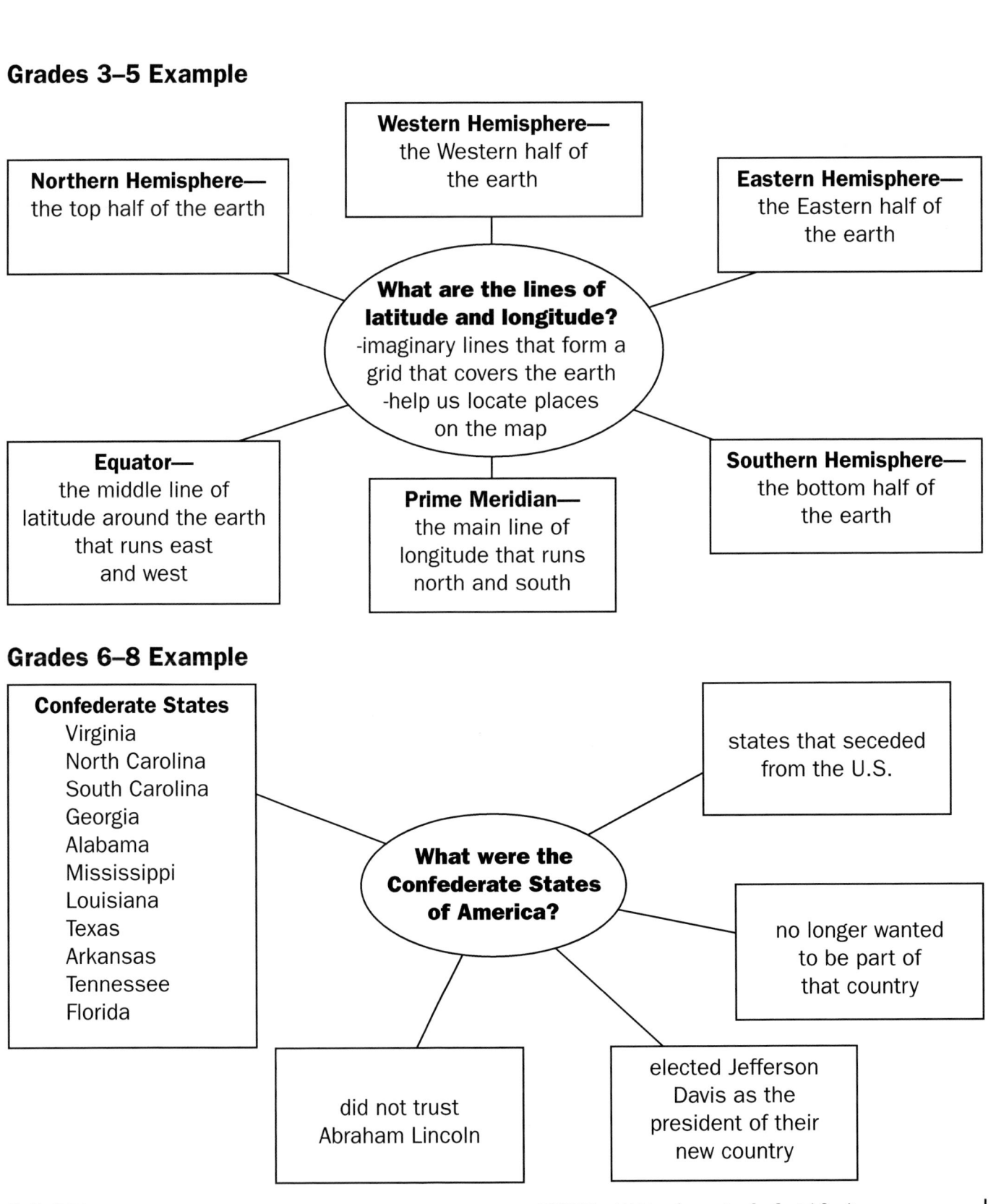

Grades 6–8 Example

Diagramming and Mapping Strategies for Social Studies *(cont.)*

Problem–Solution Map

Background Information

The Problem-Solution Map is a graphic organizer that assists students in analyzing and solving social studies problems encountered in the real world. Willis (1992) notes the advantages of teaching in units organized around a problem. Clearly identifying a problem in the real world is the first step in understanding the problem. Writing about a problem in one's own words is an effective way for students to understand the problem.

A Problem-Solution Map can be used prior to, during, or after reading. At each point this strategy can help reinforce valuable skills. Set your students up for success by explaining that no specific answers are expected. A Problem-Solution Map teaches problem-solving skills, so the more ideas that students generate the better! There are no specific answers and no right or wrong answers because a failed suggestion may turn out to provide ideas and more successful solutions.

Grade Levels/Standards Addressed

Grades 1–2 (Standard 1.1, 4.2)
Grades 3–5 (Standard 1.1, 4.7)
Grades 6–8 (Standard 1.1, 4.5)

Genres

Expository, Narrative

Stages of Writing Process

Prewrite

Activity

Determine the social studies-related problem for the focus of this lesson. Write the problem on the board or an overhead transparency. Discuss it as a class. How can it be defined as a problem? Distribute copies of the Problem-Solution Map (page 134). Instruct students to write as much as they know about this problem, using their own words. Ask the following questions to prompt students:

- What is the problem?
- Why is it a problem?
- Who or what is affected by this problem?
- When did this become a problem?
- When does this problem present itself? Daily? Weekly? Seasonally?
- Are there any obvious solutions?
- Have any solutions already been tried to solve the problem and failed?
- Is there anything that can be learned from these attempts?

Have students outline their solutions on the Problem-Solution Map. Allow them to share their ideas in small groups and discuss the expected results of this plan. If possible, students should apply their solutions, record the results, and share their findings with the class.

Diagramming and Mapping Strategies for Social Studies *(cont.)*

Problem–Solution Map *(cont.)*

Variation

Have students research social studies resources to see if the solutions they suggest have been tested or tried before. Students can share their information in a report explaining and predicting the success of their solution.

Differentiation

Pair ELLs with partners who can help them discuss and articulate their thoughts and ideas prior to filling out the Problem-Solution Map. Encourage gifted students to suggest more than one solution and to document their suggestions with research. If time allows, have gifted students present their research findings to enhance the lesson topic. Have students who are reading and writing below grade level determine possible solutions and work with partners to write out their plans to build confidence.

Problem–Solution Map *(cont.)*

Grades 1–2 Example

Directions: Write the problem in the left-hand oval. Read, research, and/or discuss with others the definition, causes, effects, and solutions.

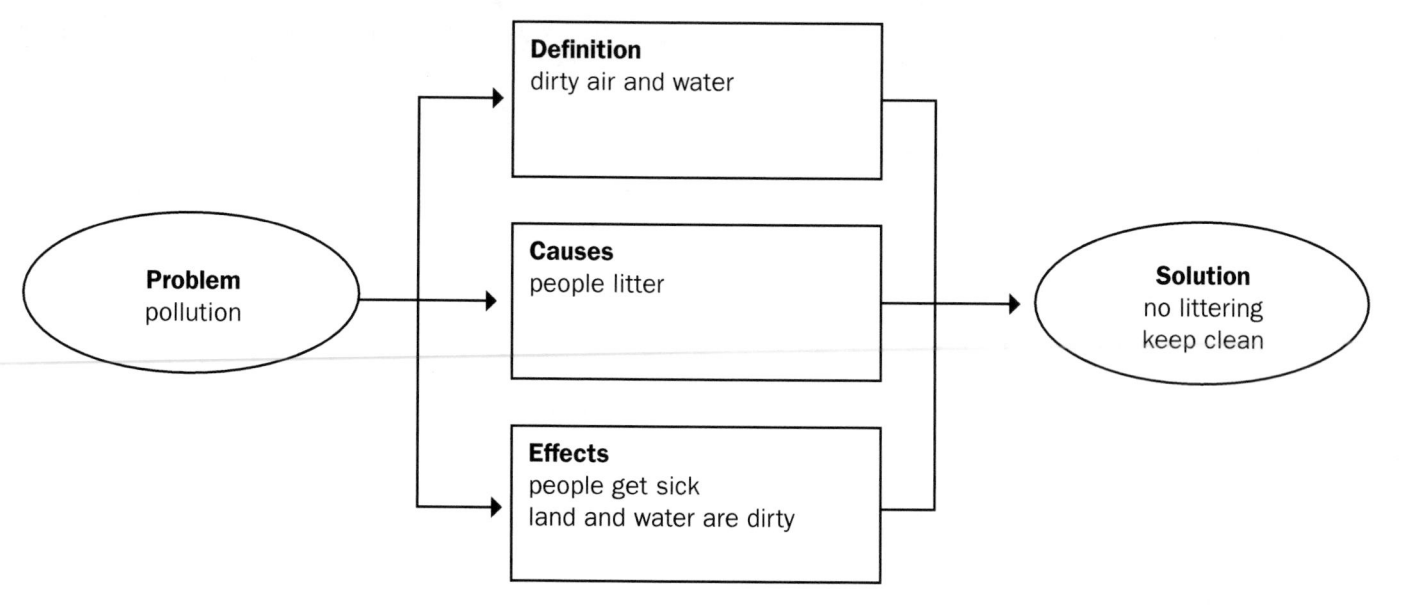

Grades 3–5 Example

Directions: Write the problem in the left-hand oval. Read, research, and/or discuss with others the definition, causes, effects, and solutions.

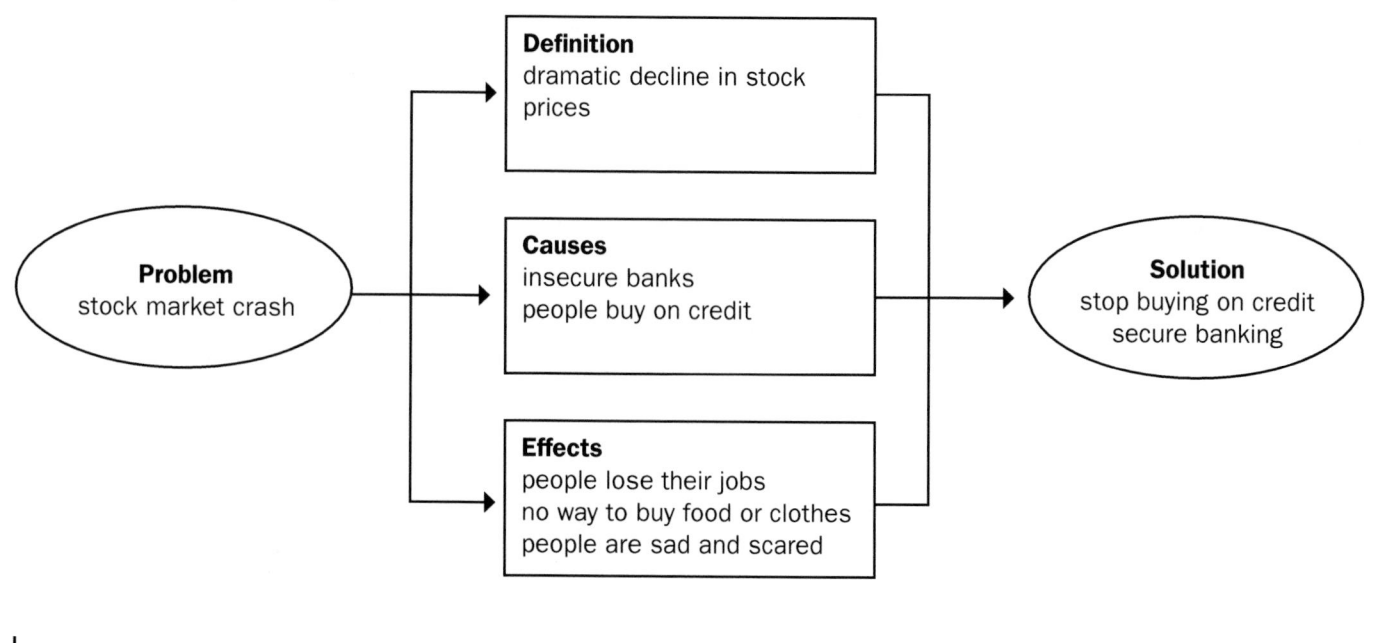

Diagramming and Mapping Strategies for Social Studies *(cont.)*

Problem-Solution Map *(cont.)*

Grades 6–8 Example

Directions: Write the problem in the left-hand oval. Read, research, and/or discuss with others the definition, causes, effects, and solutions.

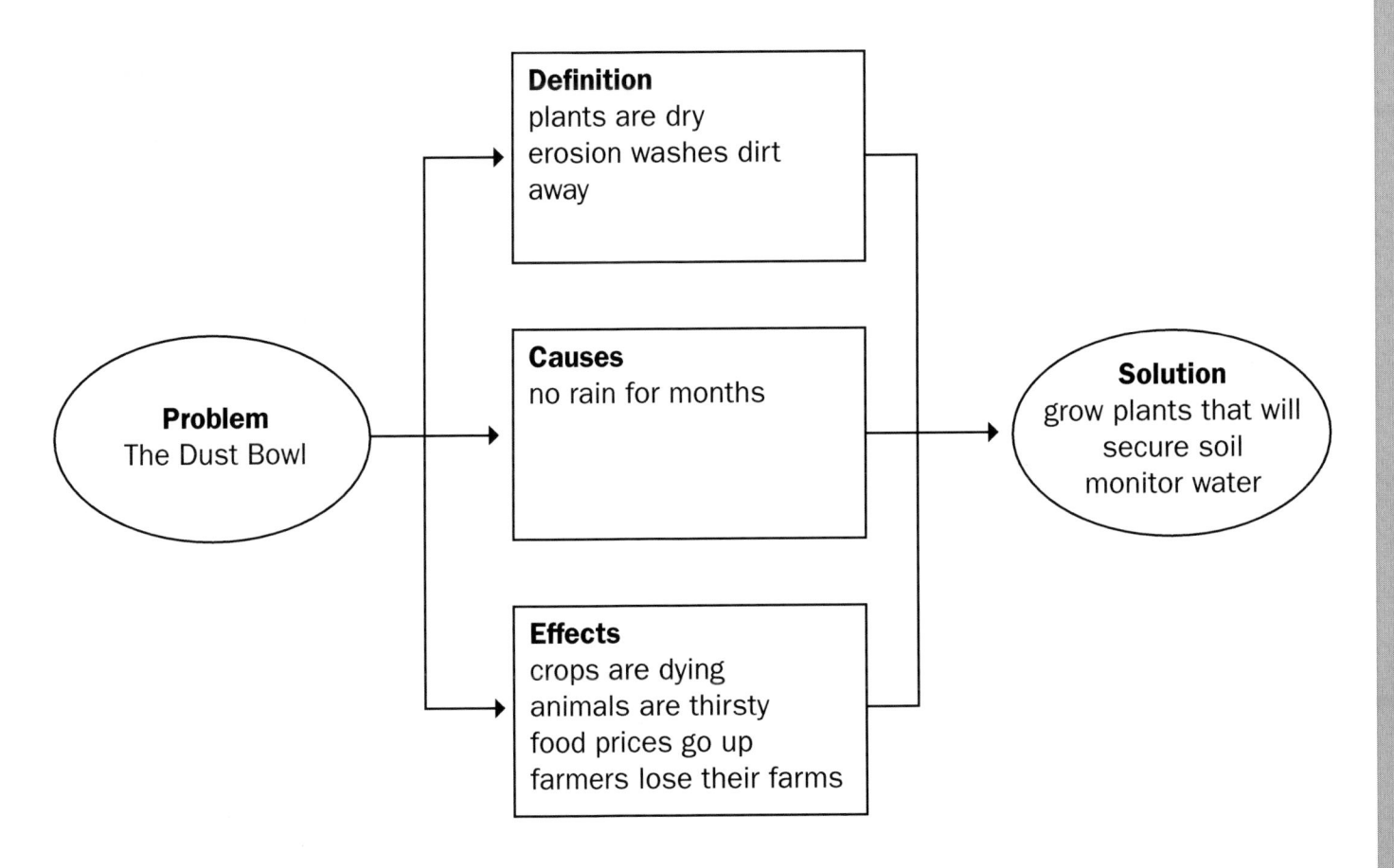

Problem–Solution Map

Directions: Write the problem in the left-hand oval. Read, research, and/or discuss with others the definition, causes, effects, and solutions.

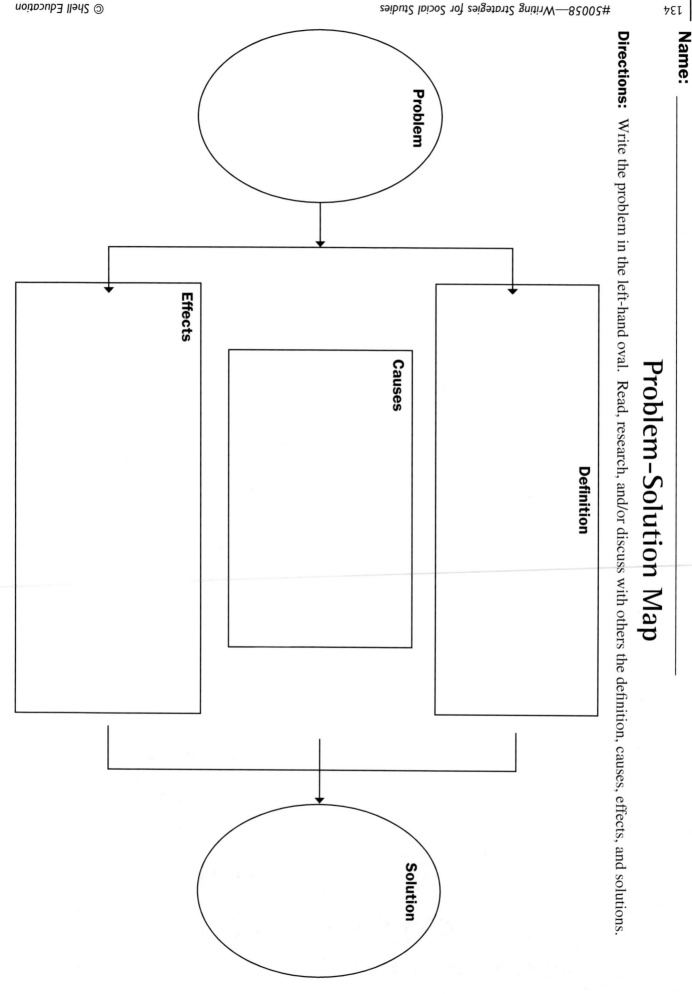

Problem

Definition

Causes

Effects

Solution

Diagramming and Mapping Strategies for Social Studies *(cont.)*

Time Order Map

Background Information

Perkins and Salomon (1988) recommend organizing instruction so that students are better able to apply knowledge and skills from one context to another. This transfer of understanding and knowledge encourages students to broaden their thinking and to apply the new information to a variety of situations. The Time Order Map helps organize information to show the passage of time. Sequence is a critical element of social studies. Capturing sequence in a graphic organizer helps students visualize the process, identify and describe each step of a sequence over time, and write more analytically about the process.

Grade Levels/Standards Addressed

Grades 1–2 (Standard 1.1, 4.2)
Grades 3–5 (Standard 1.1, 4.7)
Grades 6–8 (Standard 1.1, 4.5)

Genres

Expository

Stages of Writing Process

Prewrite

Activity

Identify a social studies topic in a text or lecture that demonstrates a sequence of events or the passage of time: key battles of a war, growth of a city, expansion of an empire, the rise of a leader, etc. Tell students that they will study the time sequence of a concept and organize the information on a graphic organizer called a Time Order Map.

Distribute copies of the Time Order Map (page 138) and conduct a short brainstorming session to activate prior knowledge about the selected concept. Assign a passage of text on this subject portraying the events over time. As students read, instruct them to add to their Time Order Map. Primary students may draw and label pictures in the Time Order Map. Encourage upper-grade students to locate and access outside information on the topic using television, radio, magazines, or newspapers, and typical sources such as social studies books and textbooks.

Differentiation

Preteach any new vocabulary words to ELLs to improve their comprehension. Also, pair them with partners to provide plenty of discussion time. Challenge gifted students to explain the cause and effect that occur at each phase of the process and to analyze the process deeper than on a surface level. Model how to complete the map for students who are reading and writing below grade level, so they understand the organization of the map. Then provide frequent feedback and prompting to keep them organized as they work. Remind these students to use the text as a tool to help them complete their map.

Diagramming and Mapping Strategies
for Social Studies (cont.)

Time Order Map (cont.)

Grades 1–2 Example
Subject: Seasons in the Northeastern United States

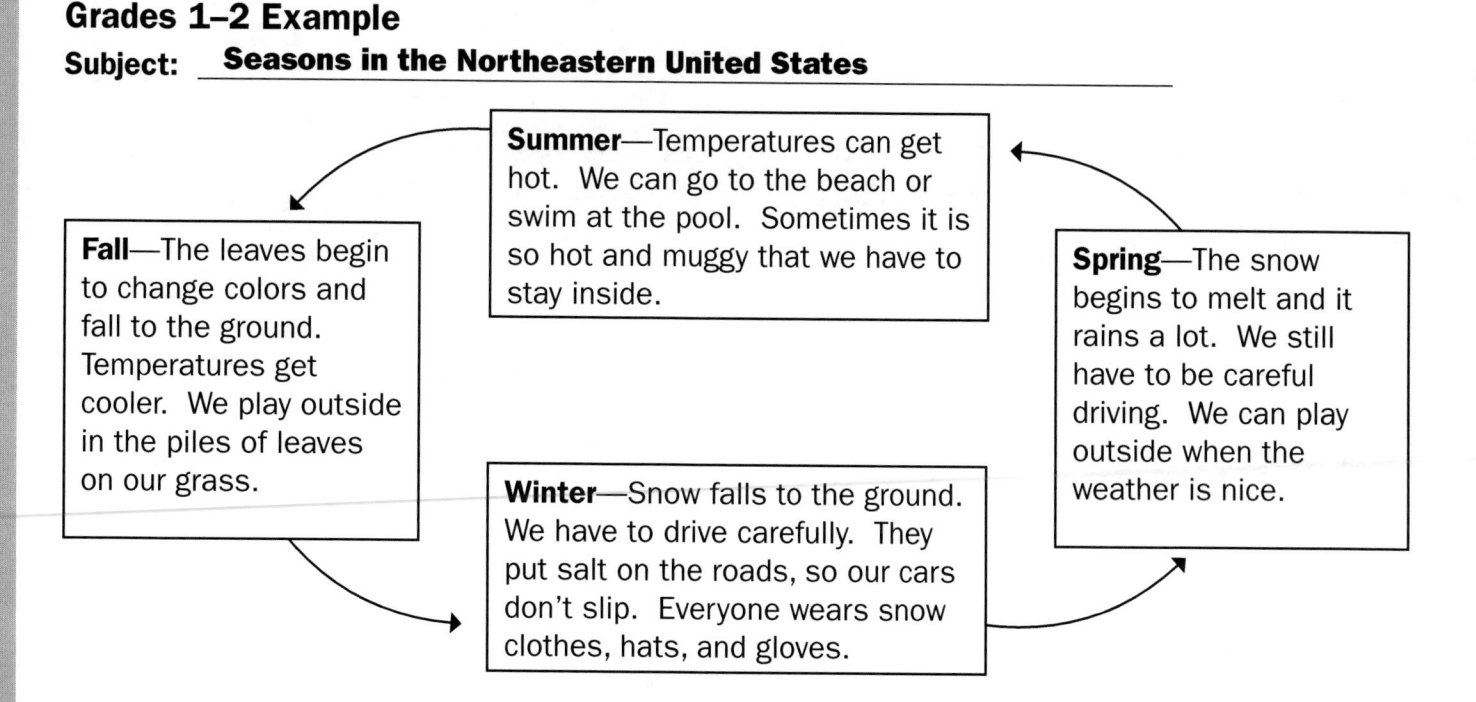

Summer—Temperatures can get hot. We can go to the beach or swim at the pool. Sometimes it is so hot and muggy that we have to stay inside.

Fall—The leaves begin to change colors and fall to the ground. Temperatures get cooler. We play outside in the piles of leaves on our grass.

Spring—The snow begins to melt and it rains a lot. We still have to be careful driving. We can play outside when the weather is nice.

Winter—Snow falls to the ground. We have to drive carefully. They put salt on the roads, so our cars don't slip. Everyone wears snow clothes, hats, and gloves.

Grades 3–5 Example
Subject: American Settlement of the West

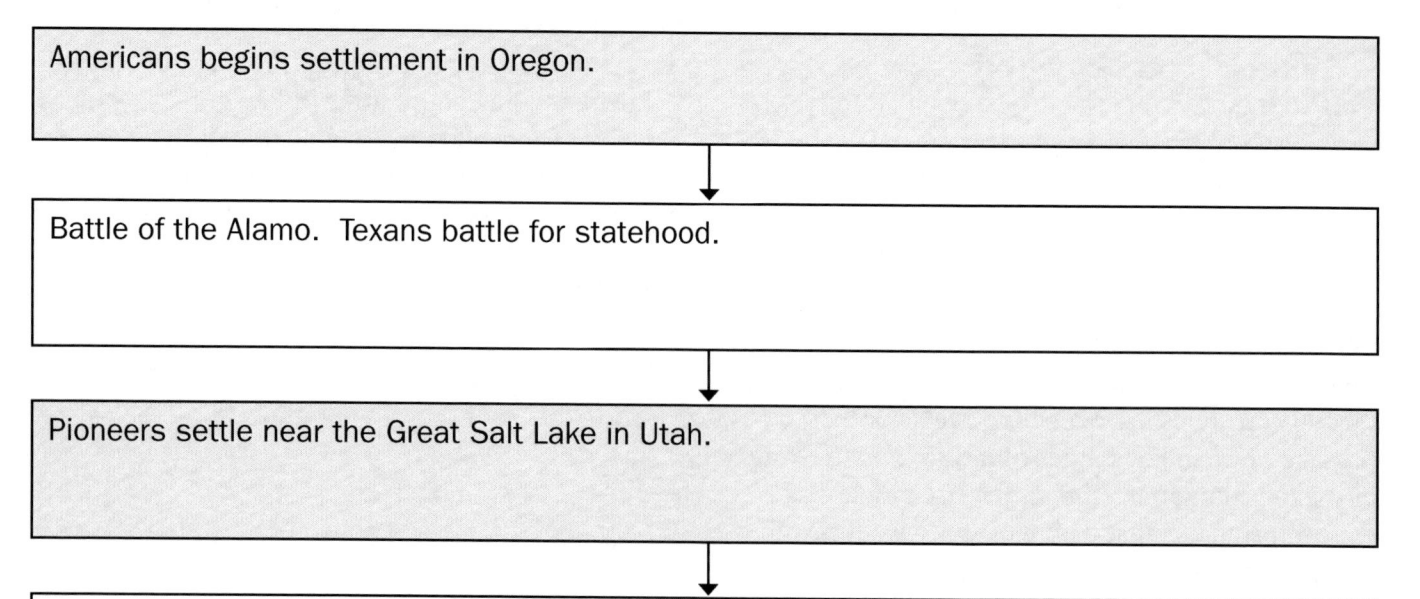

Americans begins settlement in Oregon.

Battle of the Alamo. Texans battle for statehood.

Pioneers settle near the Great Salt Lake in Utah.

Gold Rush in California draws thousands of people.

Diagramming and Mapping Strategies for Social Studies *(cont.)*

Time Order Map *(cont.)*

Grades 6–8 Example

Subject: <u>How a Bill Becomes a Law</u>

The bill must be passed through the House of Representatives and the Senate.

↓

The bill is sent to the president.

↓

The president signs or vetoes the bill. If the president signs the bill, it becomes a law. If the president vetoes the bill, it is sent back to Congress.

↓

A two-thirds vote of Congress is needed for the bill to become a law.

Name: _____

Time Order Map

Directions: Use this map to show the sequence of events. Write the first event in the top box, and the second event in the second box. Continue until you have described the entire chain of events.

Subject: _____

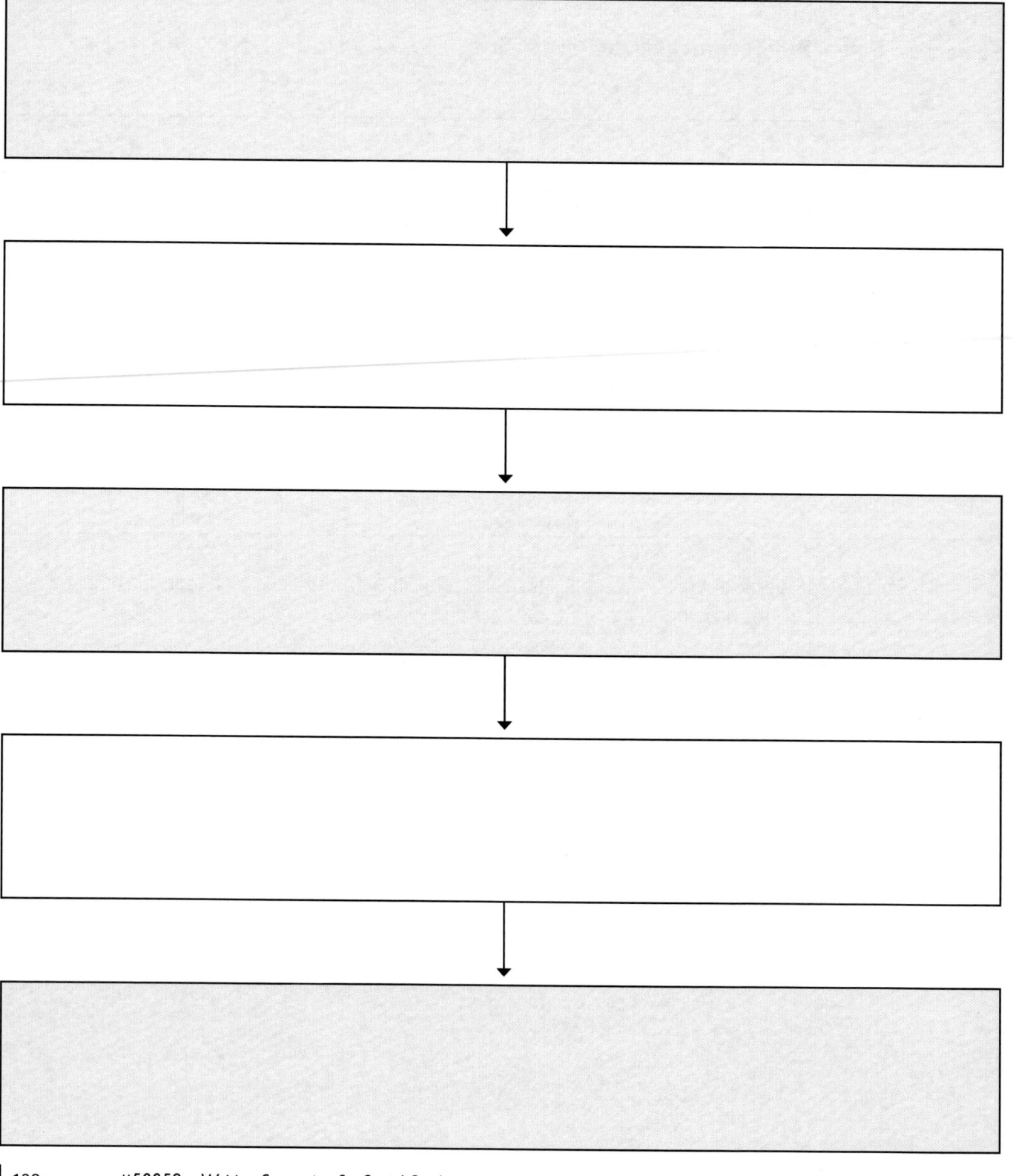

Name: _____

Time Order Map

Directions: Use this map to show how a sequence of events happens in a circular manner. Write the events in order in the boxes.

Topic: _____

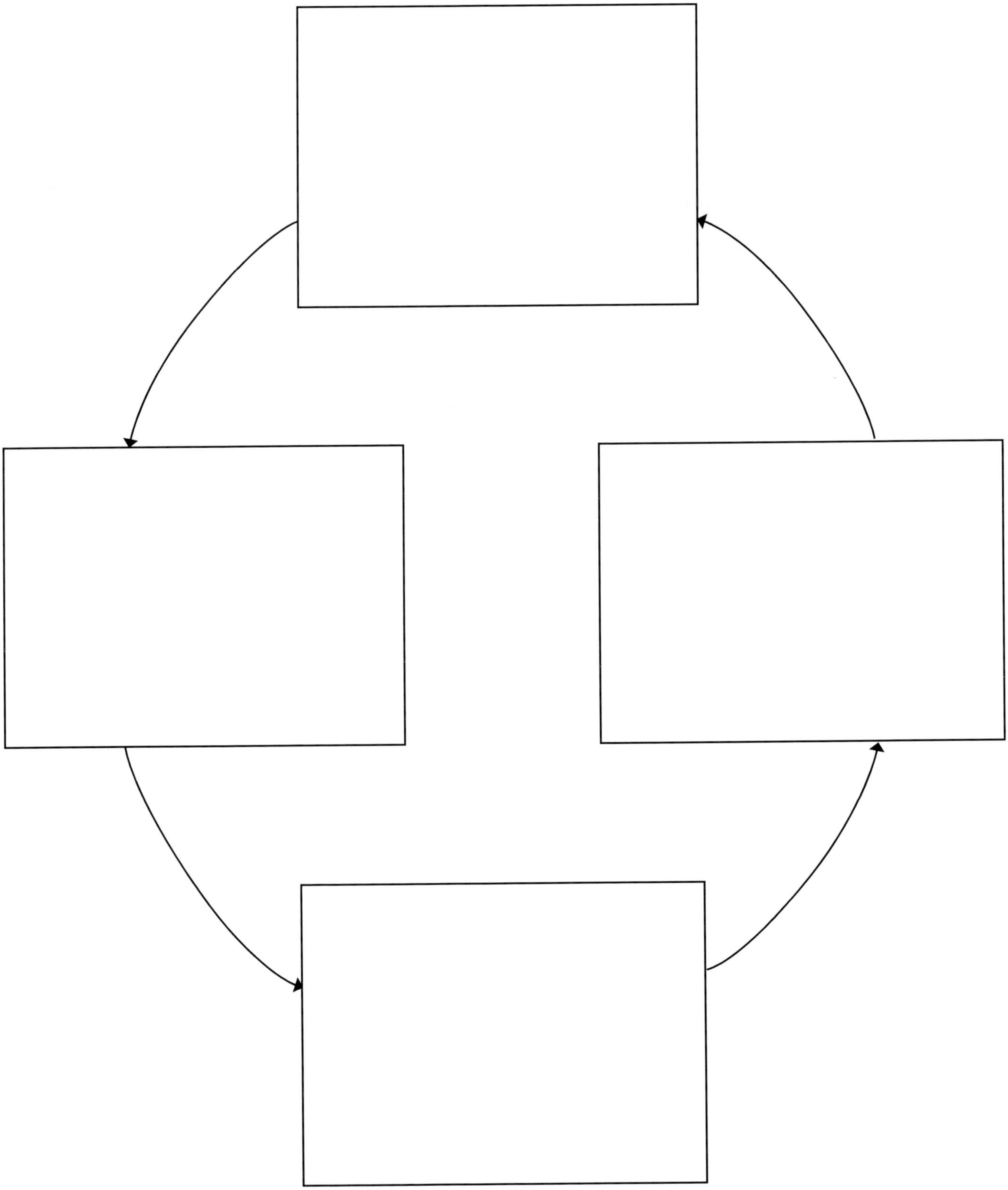

Authoring in Social Studies

This book has previously established the strong connection between reading and writing. The quote from Gay Su Pinnell in the article "Success of Children at Risk in a Program That Combines Writing and Reading" bears repeating: "As children read and write they make the connections that form their basic understandings about both. Learning in one area enhances learning in the other. There is ample evidence to suggest that the processes are inseparable and that we should examine pedagogy in the light of these relationships. Hence, the two activities should be integrated in instructional settings. Teachers need to create supportive situations in which children have opportunities to explore the whole range of literacy learning, and they need to design instruction that helps children make connections between reading and writing."

Reading and writing are critical to all learning. Writing to apply new knowledge can be more challenging for students because they need to not only understand the content and be able to process it at a higher level, but also communicate it using the strategies of the writing process, the features of the chosen genre, and the conventions of the grade level. Through authoring, students can make personal connections with the new content information they are learning.

Santa, Havens, and Harrison (1996) make several key points with regard to this connection.

1. **Writing helps students become more active learners of the social studies content.** Creating writing pieces that utilize social studies content knowledge requires students to think more deeply about the content, analyze it, and reconstruct it into a piece of writing.

2. **Writing assists students in understanding the complexities of social studies.** Writing can provide opportunities for students to analyze new concepts, internalize new vocabulary, and explore patterns and relationships between concepts.

3. **Writing forces learners to organize their thinking and to evaluate if they have understood a concept.** In order to communicate in writing, students must carefully consider how to approach the writing activity. For example, students who are asked to write a newspaper article about a current event must not only organize the content information that they intend to include but also meld it with the style appropriate for the genre. Within the framework of the genre, students must decide how best to communicate their information.

4. **One cannot write about something one does not understand (Santa, Havens, and Harrison 1996).** The process of creating a clear explanation of a concept will challenge students to think carefully about the best way to explain it. In working through this challenge, students can develop a deeper understanding of the concept.

Authoring Strategies for Social Studies

Guided Writing Procedure

Background Information

The Guided Writing Procedure (Smith and Bean 1980) uses writing as a vehicle for activating students' prior knowledge and synthesizing existing and new information in social studies. Students brainstorm about a topic to lay a foundation for building new social studies content knowledge, then analyze the information for patterns and relationships to create an outline, just as good writers do during the prewriting phase. After writing a paragraph, students compare their work with that of the social studies textbook, article, or trade book to look for similarities and differences and opportunities to add or change information.

Grade Levels/Standards Addressed

Grades 3–5 (Standard 1.1–1.2)
Grades 6–8 (Standard 1.1–1.2)

Genres

Expository, Summary, Narrative, Persuasive

Stages of Writing Process

Prewrite, Draft, Revise

Activity

Write on the board the key concept for the reading lesson. Ask students to brainstorm everything they know about that concept, and write their responses on the board. Remind them that there are no "wrong" ideas in brainstorming. Then review the brainstormed ideas as a class, decide which of them are major points and which are supporting details, and create a simple outline as a prewriting strategy. Provide time for students to draft a paragraph or two using the class outline. Next, have students read the assigned text and analyze their work against the social studies text: They should see how well the class outline matches the social studies text, look for similarities and differences between their own paragraph(s) and the text, and identify information that could be added or deleted from their writing, based on the social studies text.

Differentiation

Scaffold notes or create an outline for ELLs to use as they write their paragraphs. Model the strategy and provide examples of completed paragraphs for these students to refer to. Have gifted students write more than a paragraph, perhaps a report, on the topic. Conduct writing conferences with students reading and writing below grade level to explicitly instruct how to use notes from the prewriting stage to create a draft. Also, provide models of good paragraphs and spend time in the conferences analyzing the good writing traits shown in the examples. Use the students' work to guide them through analyzing their writing and the text for similarities and differences. Understanding and being able to recognize good writing helps these students become better writers themselves.

Authoring Strategies for Social Studies *(cont.)*

Guided Writing Procedure *(cont.)*

Grades 3–5 Example

Concept: Revolutionary War

Key Points/Supporting Details: British, battles, uniforms, ocean, ships, wounded, New England, colonists, weapons

Sample Paragraph:

The Revolutionary War was a difficult time for the colonists of New England. Many battles took place between the British and the colonists. The colonists did not have the fancy uniforms of the British, nor did they have the same weapons. Many colonists were wounded and killed in these battles. The ocean separated the colonists from the British, but they came on their large ships anyway.

Grades 6–8 Example

Concept: World War II

Key Points/Supporting Details: Allies, Axis Powers, Hitler, Nazi, Jews, Concentration Camps, D-Day

Sample Paragraph:

World War II split the world in half. Many countries working together formed the Allies while a different group of countries formed the Axis Powers. These were two opposing groups. Hitler led the Nazi army in an attempt to take over Europe. He ordered millions of Jews to concentration camps where millions were exterminated. The Allies finally came on D-Day to rescue the Jews and the many others.

Authoring Strategies for Social Studies *(cont.)*

Reading-Writing Workbench

Background Information

The Reading-Writing Workbench (Tierney, Caplan, Ehri, Healy, Hurdlow 1989) strategy incorporates writing as a pre-reading activity and teaches students how to use resources as they read and write. After students explore their own experiences relating to a theme introduced in the social studies text, they read, discuss, and compare their ideas with their peers and those of professional authors. The "workbench" refers to the way the teacher coordinates the use of and interaction with scientific, as well as other, resources.

Grade Levels/Standards Addressed

Grades 3–5 (Standard 1.1–1.2)
Grades 6–8 (Standard 1.1–1.2)

Genres

Expository, Summary

Stages of Writing Process

Prewrite, Draft, Revise

Activity

Lead a class discussion about the key concept of the lesson. Ask students to share any personal experiences or any background knowledge they have relating to this concept. Next, have students independently write about their experiences. Allow a few minutes for students to share their writing, as well as the techniques they used as the author. Identify the resources available on this topic: social studies books, television programs, newspaper articles, etc. Encourage students to bring in the resources they find to share with the class, and, if possible, make these resources available to the students to read. Ask students in small groups to read their writing and compare it to that of the resources your class has obtained. Here are some questions for students to consider:

- How does your writing compare with other published texts on the same topic?

- How can you incorporate these ideas into your own writing?

- How did you begin and end the piece of writing while maintaining the interest of the audience?

- How did you incorporate social studies facts and still make it interesting and authentic?

In conclusion, allow time for students to use group comments to reflect on what they have learned through this process.

Differentiation

When working as a whole class, make sure the ideas and background knowledge shared by the students are easy to understand for ELLs. This is important when students begin to write about the topic. Repeat and rephrase what students say to make it easier for ELLs to comprehend. Gifted students will benefit from an assignment to incorporate several sources into their writing. Show students how to cite sources in their writing. Provide plenty of discussion time for students reading and writing below grade level. Hold independent writing conferences as necessary to provide support for these students.

Authoring Strategies for Social Studies *(cont.)*

Reading-Writing Workbench *(cont.)*

Grades 3–5 Example

Social Studies Topic: __Columbus's Voyage__

Background Knowledge/Ideas:

I know that Columbus was an explorer.
He discovered America.
He sailed on the Nina, the Pinta, and the Santa Maria.

Student Writing:

Columbus set sail in August of 1492. He left from Spain on three ships named the Nina, the Pinta, and the Santa Maria. He had ninety sailors with him. In the early morning of October 12, the crew discovered land. It was America. He thought he had discovered this new land on behalf of those in Europe, but the American Indians had already discovered the land. Columbus found them living there.

Grades 6–8 Example

Social Studies Topic: __Pigments for Clothing and Textiles__

Background Knowledge/Ideas:

Pigments are made from plants.
People from long ago used to make pigments to die cloth.
Pigments are still used today.

Student Writing:

Through the years, pigments have been made from many different items. Some pigments have been made from crushing rocks, or from smashing plants and leaves. These colors were mixed with animal fats to create a smooth mixture to spread on homes or even bodies. New colors were made by blending two pigments together. Many people died making pigments because the pigments were toxic and the people didn't know that.

Name: _____

Reading-Writing Workbench

Social Studies Topic: _____

Background Knowledge/Ideas:

_____

_____

Student Writing:

_____

_____

_____

_____

_____

_____

How does your writing compare with other published texts on the same topic?

_____

_____

How can you incorporate these ideas into your own writing?

_____

_____

How did you begin and end the piece of writing while maintaining the interest of the audience?

_____

_____

How did you incorporate social studies facts and still make it interesting and authentic?

_____

Authoring Strategies for Social Studies *(cont.)*

Author's Chair

Background Information

The Author's Chair strategy (Blackburn 1982; Boutwell 1983; Calkins 1983; Graves 1983; Graves and Hansen 1983) provides student writers with feedback on their writing. It has also been called peer conferencing. Researchers and educators continue to confirm the strong connections between reading and writing and between authors and readers. The focus of the Author's Chair strategy is to provide feedback to students on their writing: acknowledging its good qualities, making specific suggestions for improvement, and asking thought-provoking questions of the student authors.

Grade Levels/Standards Addressed

Grades 1–2 (Standard 1.4)
Grades 3–5 (Standard 1.4)
Grades 6–8 (Standard 1.4)

Genres

Expository, Summary, Narrative, Persuasive

Stages of Writing Process

Revise

Activity

Ask students to select a social studies writing piece and place them in groups of no more than four. Give each group the following tasks:

- Students take turns reading their pieces of writing aloud.

- Group members listen intently and share their feedback.

- Once all members of the group have shared their writing and received feedback, instruct students to read about their writing topics in social studies texts and other social studies resources. *How does their writing compare with professional writers? What can be learned about writing from professional writers? What can be learned about how the authors structure and organize their writing?*

- Allow time for students to edit and revise their writing. Students can use this time to incorporate into their writing suggestions from peers as well as ideas from professional writers. If time permits, allow small groups to meet again and repeat the strategy.

Variation

With primary grade students, conduct the strategy as a whole class. Choose one or two students to read their writing pieces to the class, and then ask the class to provide feedback. Remind students to offer specific comments (see pages 147–148 for examples).

Differentiation

Hold individual writing conferences with ELLs and students reading and writing below grade level to provide direct instruction and specific feedback. Consider using a lower-level text as a model so that the reading level does not hinder their abilities to analyze writing qualities. These students can join groups when it is time to peruse social studies materials and texts. Group gifted students with others who will challenge their writing skills. Ask them to share the techniques they learned from a professional writer and how they plan to incorporate these techniques into their own writing.

Authoring Strategies for Social Studies *(cont.)*

Author's Chair *(cont.)*

Grades 1–2 Example

Student Writing Sample:

Most of the people who traveled to America became farmers. Some of these people decided to live in the cities. The towns needed workers with many skills. The workers were able to have their own land and have a good life.

Class Comments:

Student 1: Your paragraph has a good sequence. It makes sense to me.

Student 2: You could explain what kinds of skills the workers had to give it more detail.

Student 3: All of your sentences are complete.

Grades 3–5 Example

Student Writing Sample:

It took four months of travel by sea to reach America. Many of the new settlers died on the trip. The three ships finally reached Chesapeake Bay. They chose to settle along the banks of the river. They named their settlement Jamestown after their king. They first few years in Jamestown were very hard. Many of the settlers got sick. It was a difficult beginning.

Class Comments:

Student 1: You have a lot of good information. It sounds like you did a lot of research.

Student 2: I think you could add more detail to extend your sentences.

Student 3: Last week, we talked about how informational writing includes transition words and phrases. It might be easier to read if you added some transitions.

Authoring Strategies for Social Studies *(cont.)*

Author's Chair *(cont.)*

Grades 6–8 Example

Student Writing Sample:

Daniel Boone was a famous hunter in the 1700s. He loved to explore and became restless if he was not out in the wilderness. He felt crowded when more and more cabins were built. He was already ready for an adventure. His rifle brought him safety and food, as well as other supplies. Daniel Boone was called on many times to explore the great frontier.

Class Comments:

Student 1: You have a topic sentence, but you might want to try to make it more creative. Maybe start with a question before the sentence you already wrote.

Student 2: The paragraph was well organized because you started with a topic sentence and then added the supporting details. It might be easier to follow if you incorporated some transition words.

Student 3: You included a lot of information, but your senteces are mostly simple sentences. You might want to start your sentences with something besides "he" and "his" to make the writing sound more interesting.

Authoring Strategies for Social Studies *(cont.)*

Read, Encode, Annotate, Ponder

Background Information

The purpose of the Read, Encode, Annotate, Ponder (REAP) strategy (Eanet and Manzo 1976) is to develop in students a greater understanding of the author's role in writing and to improve their reading comprehension. REAP helps students build a bridge between the social studies text and their own words to enable them to communicate their understanding of the text.

Grade Levels/Standards Addressed

Grades 3–5 (Standard 1.4, 1.11)
Grades 6–8 (Standard 1.4, 1.12)

Genres

Expository, Persuasive

Stages of Writing Process

Draft

Activity

Distribute the REAP strategy sheet (page 152) prior to reading a selected social studies text. The steps students follow for this activity come from the acronym:

R—Read and understand the author's ideas. After students read the assigned text, have them discuss the contents of the text with partners, small groups, or in a whole class discussion.

E—Encode the author's words into their own words. Have the students put in their own words what the text passage says. They should be able to do this without having to reread the material as they talk about it. They should become familiar enough with the text to discuss it comfortably. *What is the main idea? What is the concept being presented? Can I explain what the author is saying?*

A—Annotate what they are reading. Annotation is not just a summary of what students have read. Instead, it is an extension of or elaboration on the text. Prompt students with these questions:

- What is the author's opinion on the subject? How can you tell?
- What is the problem being presented in the text? What are some possible solutions?
- Analyze the writing in the text. Is it clear? Could it be improved? Is it creative in how it is presented? Does it need any clarification or additions?
- What is the author's purpose or intention for writing?
- What can you learn from the author's writing that will help your own writing?

P—Pondering means that students must think about what they have written. Does it make sense? Does it complement or differ from what was said in the text?

Differentiation

Scaffold notes or create an outline for ELLs as they do their writing. Provide examples of writing samples for them. Have gifted students write more than a paragraph, such as a report, on the topic. Explicitly model for students reading and writing below grade level how to respond in each of the sections. Also, spend individual time in a writing conference analyzing their own writing.

Authoring Strategies for Social Studies (cont.)

Read, Encode, Annotate, Ponder (cont.)

Grades 3–5 Example

Study Topic/Reading Assignment: _____ **The Civil War** _____

R—Read and understand the author's ideas. Do you understand what you are reading? Do you understand all the words? Do you need help with understanding anything?
I am reading a book about the Civil War. I know it was a battle between the Northern and the Southern states in America. I don't understand how or why Americans would want to kill each other. I also don't know what the word 'confederate' means.
E—Encode what the author's words in their own words. What is the author saying? What is the main idea or concept being presented? What did you learn by reading this passage? Explain it in your own words.
The main idea of this passage is that the North decided to attack Richmond, Virginia, which was the capital of the Southern states. The author is trying to explain why the Northern states thought this would be a good idea. The Northern states didn't realize how prepared the Southern states would be.
A—Annotate what you read. What is the author's opinion on the subject? How can you tell? What is the problem being presented in the text? What are some possible solutions? What can you learn from the author's writing that will help your own?
I think the author agreed with the Northern states. He seems to talk about how organized they were compared to South. The North had uniforms and trained generals and soldiers. The Southern states were not as well organized. The author did a good job of comparing and contrasting the two armies.
P—Ponder what you have written. Does it make sense? Would someone else understand what you have written? Is it accurate? Do you need to change anything? Did you use your own words?
I used my own words and I think that someone else reading it would understand. I don't think I have enough information, though. I need to read more about the Civil War because my writing doesn't share enough information.

Authoring Strategies for Social Studies (cont.)

Read, Encode, Annotate, Ponder (cont.)

Grades 6–8 Example

Study Topic/Reading Assignment: <u>**The Vietnam War**</u>

R—Read and understand the author's ideas. Do you understand what you are reading? Do you understand all the words? Do you need help with understanding anything?
The article I read was about the Vietnam War. There are a lot of new words, but most of them are because Vietnam is a different country with a different language. Many of the words that are hard to understand are words for cities, towns, and places.
E—Encode the author's words into your own words. What is the author saying? What is the main idea or concept being presented? What did you learn by reading this passage? Explain it in your own words.
The Vietnam War was a very controversial war. Today, the United States is still split over whether or not the United States should have gotten involved in the war. It was also a difficult war to fight. Many U.S. soldiers were injured and killed during the war and there were many protesters who were fighting and saying that we should not be fighting this war.
A—Annotate what you read. What is the author's opinion on the subject? How can you tell? What is the problem being presented in the text? What are some possible solutions? What can you learn from the author's writing that will help your own?
The author is trying to encourage people to believe that the Vietnam War was a waste of time, a waste of people, and a waste of money. I can tell he doesn't agree with the United States fighting that war. I am having a hard time deciding what the right thing is. I think it's because I don't understand all the reasons for the war. The author persuaded me to think about these things.
P—Ponder what you have written. Does it make sense? Would someone else understand what you have written? Is it accurate? Do you need to change anything? Did you use your own words?
I used my own words and I think that someone else reading it would understand. I don't think I have enough information, though. I need to read more about the Vietnam War to present a more thorough piece of writing.

Name: _____

Read, Encode, Annotate, Ponder

Study Topic/Reading Assignment: _____

R – Read and understand the author's ideas. Do you understand what you are reading? Do you understand all the words?   Do you need help with understanding anything?

_____

_____

_____

_____

E – Encode the author's words into your own words. What is the author saying? What is the main idea or concept being presented? What did you learn by reading this passage? Explain it in your own words.

_____

_____

_____

_____

A – Annotate what you read. What is the author's opinion on the subject? How can you tell? What is the problem presented in the text? What are some possible solutions? What can you learn from the author's writing that will help your own?

_____

_____

_____

_____

P – Ponder what you have written. Does it make sense? Would someone else understand what you have written? Is it accurate? Do you need to change anything? Did you use your own words?

_____

_____

_____

_____

Summarizing in Social Studies

The Challenge of Summarizing

Summarizing improves readers' abilities to locate the main ideas and supporting details, identify and omit unnecessary details and redundant materials, remember what is read, analyze text structure and see how ideas are related, generalize details, clarify meaning, take notes, and rethink what they have read so that they can process it more deeply.

Summarizing is, to a certain extent, like a scientific process. When students summarize their reading, they distill large sections of text, extract the most essential information, and then create a coherent, more concise text that relates the same information as the original text. In order to effectively summarize, writers must be able to identify the main ideas and differentiate important information from unimportant information in order to stress the most vital parts and minimize less relevant details.

Condensing text so that the substance of a reading selection is in brief form is no easy task and often leads to artificial, awkward language and organization. Summaries should be revised, as with any finished writing product, so they sound more natural when read. When students translate the ideas they have read into their own words, they can more easily retrieve that information to accomplish a learning task. Students must use their own words to form connections across the concepts and relate the concepts to their own prior knowledge and experiences.

The Steps in Summarizing

Students need to remember three important elements to summarize effectively. Students must keep the information in their summaries brief, identify the most important ideas, and mention some supporting details.

The Main Idea

One of the skills involved in summarizing is expressing the main idea. In order to summarize, students must be able to identify the key concepts or chief topic of a passage, a paragraph, and a sentence. The main idea is the central thought, but it can be overlooked when teaching students how to summarize. Therefore, students need instruction and practice in communicating the main idea, as it is the one idea to which all other sentences in a passage relate.

Quick and Easy Main Idea Activities

The following activities are fast, easy ways to highlight how to locate the main idea in reading passages (Dechant 1991):

- Have students categorize objects or words from a passage. This helps them recognize the main ideas.

- Instruct students to identify the main idea of a group of sentences by underlining key words.

- Ask students to locate the topic sentence or the key sentence that best identifies the main idea of a paragraph. Remind them to use these as models for their own topic sentences when they write.

- Have students write a title for a paragraph or a passage. Have the students read a newspaper story on a social studies topic and remove the title. Ask them to give the story an appropriate title and then compare it to the actual title.

Summary-Writing Strategies for Social Studies

GIST

Background Information

The GIST strategy (Moore, Moore, Cunningham, and Cunningham 1994) helps students get the "gist" of the social studies text in order to write a clear, concise summary in 20 words or less. As students progress in school, teachers begin to limit the number of words or pages for writing assignments. This strategy strengthens students' writing skills by teaching them to eliminate unnecessary information and determine the key points of the text. Therefore, each word used in a GIST must have great importance. Using GIST is valuable not only when summarizing a reading passage but also when writing the summary of a multi-paragraph essay. To prepare students, review the features of a high-quality summary.

Grade Levels/Standards Addressed

Grades 3–5 (Standard 1.1–1.2, 1.11)
Grades 6–8 (Standard 1.1–1.2, 1.12)

Genres

Expository, Summary

Stages of Writing Process

Prewrite, Draft, Revise

Activity

Assign a social studies passage for students that is fairly short—no more than three paragraphs—and easy to read, then distribute the GIST activity sheet (page 156). Ask students to identify the main points of the passage and write these on the board or a transparency. Ask them to list the supporting details or statements to complete a prewriting outline. Next, instruct students to use the class outline to write a summary of no more than 20 words and edit and revise it, as good writers do. Put students in groups of no more than four to share their paragraphs and receive feedback, which they can use to revise and edit the summaries. As students become more proficient in using this strategy, gradually eliminate the group and/or whole-class work so that they eventually write and edit their summaries independently.

Differentiation

While working as a class during the modeling phase, use simple vocabulary and discuss the meaning of this vocabulary so that ELLs can understand. Use opportunities to rephrase and repeat these terms. Check for understanding before moving on to the writing phase. For gifted students, assign longer passages to read and challenge them to write shorter summaries. Allow students reading and writing below grade level to work with partners to identify the important ideas and words. If necessary, lengthen the word limit on their summaries.

Summary-Writing Strategies for Social Studies *(cont.)*

GIST *(cont.)*

Grades 3–5 Example

Text Passage

During the 1850s, America saw a large growth of cities. Most of the cities were in the Northeast by this time. Many of these cities were fast growing. Transportation played a big role in cities growing. The railroads made it possible for people to travel all over the United States. Factories also drew more people into the cities. Factories provided jobs for many people. Most of these were small factories, but there were plenty of them. There was a desire to keep moving, learning, and growing by the American people. Many inventions were discovered during this time.

Key Points

America, growth, 1850s
> transportation
> factories
> progress
> travel
> work

Summary (No more than 20 words)

The 1850s were a time of growth and progress in America. Transportation and factories allowed people to travel and work.

Grades 6–8 Example

Text Passage

The Industrial Revolution brought about many changes for the American people. It was a time of growth and progress. It brought more goods to people. It provided many jobs for people. The factories now needed skilled workers that could run machines and run the large companies. This also put many people out of work. The new machines were now doing the jobs that people used to do. The factory worker worked at least 10 to 12 hours a day. It was not uncommon to work six days a week. It was also not uncommon to have children working these long and hard hours in the factory. The conditions in the factories were not always safe. Many people died from injuries. Labor unions began to spring up as a way to help the workers.

Key Points

Industrial Revolution
> jobs
> skilled workers
> conditions
> labor unions

Summary (No more than 20 words)

The Industrial Revolution brought about the need for skilled workers. New labor unions helped create better conditions for workers.

Name: _____

GIST

Directions: After reading the first section of a text, write down the important ideas and create a summary. Then read the second section of text and condense all the information into a combined summary.

Important Ideas from Section 1:

_____   _____   _____

_____   _____   _____

_____   _____   _____

_____   _____   _____

Summary:

_____

_____

_____

Summary-Writing Strategies for Social Studies *(cont.)*

Key Words

Background Information

Key Words (Hoyt 1999) is a summary strategy that is better suited to younger students because it does not limit the number of words used in a summary. It provides greater scaffolding to support students in creating a clear, concise summary. Before summarizing, students are asked to simply identify the key words from the text. Those words are then used to compose the summary. Unlike the GIST strategy, Key Words does not limit the number of words in the summary. Key Words can also be effective for older students who are learning to write summaries in multi-paragraph compositions.

Grade Levels/Standards Addressed

Grades 1–2 (Standard 1.1–1.2)
Grades 3–5 (Standard 1.1–1.2, 1.11)

Genres

Expository, Summary, Persuasive

Stages of Writing Process

Prewrite, Draft, Revise

Activity

Explain that students are to look for the main ideas, or key words, as they read a selected social studies text. Give students scrap paper, sticky notes, or notebook paper on which to write the key words. After the reading, call on students to share their words, discuss the significance of each one, and justify their choices to develop a class list of the key words from the text. Model and discuss how to organize, rearrange, and delete duplicate key words as needed. Then write a summary using the key words, either by modeling the entire process or using guided writing techniques (see pages 141–142 for Guided Writing). Model for students how to edit and revise the summary, so it flows naturally. Provide adequate guided practice time before allowing students to write a summary independently.

Differentiation

Preview the text and preteach any new vocabulary words for ELLs to improve their comprehension. Guide these students in a small group to develop their summaries. Give gifted students reading materials that are appropriate for their reading level and challenge them by limiting the number of words used in their summaries. Scaffold for students reading and writing below grade level by modeling how to identify key words to look for as they read.

Summary-Writing Strategies for Social Studies (cont.)

Key Words (cont.)

Grades 1–2 Example

Text Passage

Inventions help countries grow and progress. Some of the most important inventions in our country are still around today.

Key Words:

inventions

Summary:

Inventions make a big difference in our lives.

Grades 3–5 Example

Text Passage:

The Constitution did not go into effect until nine states had ratified or approved it. Many states approved it quickly, while other states had serious debates over it. The Constitution was finally ratified by eleven states in July of 1788 when a bill of rights was promised.

Key Words:

Constitution, ratified, approved

Summary:

The Constitution needed to be approved by a majority of the states. There was a lot of discussion about it.

Summary-Writing Strategies for Social Studies (cont.)

Guided Reading and Summarizing Procedure

Background Information

The Guided Reading and Summarizing Procedure (GRASP) (Hayes 1989, as cited by Ryder and Graves 2003; Lenski, Wham, and Johns 1999) teaches students to summarize independently. Students learn to recall, organize, and self-correct information before composing a summary through teacher modeling. Ryder and Graves (2003) suggest that the students and teacher subsequently write summaries individually, then compare and contrast the students' summaries to that of the teacher. According to Ryder and Graves (2003), Hayes (1989) suggests the teacher revise his or her summary based on the students' suggestions and make a visible record of these changes to make the revision process more concrete for students.

Grade Levels/Standards Addressed

Grades 3–5 (Standard 1.1–1.2, 1.11)
Grades 6–8 (Standard 1.1–1.2, 1.12)

Genres

Expository, Summary, Persuasive

Stages of Writing Process

Prewrite, Draft, Revise

Activity

Explain to students that they will use the Guided Reading and Summarizing Procedure to help them summarize the information in a text. Emphasize the importance of learning how to summarize text and knowing when summarizing is needed. When students have finished reading the selected social studies text, have them share what they remember. Write their comments on the board or an overhead transparency. Then have students read the text again, this time looking for any information that they missed, that can be elaborated on, or that is inaccurate. Make changes as needed, then organize the ideas into main ideas and details. Using this class outline, model writing a summary passage for the students. Read through the summary as a class to edit and revise it, so it flows naturally and contains all the important points from the text passage. After learning how to use the GRASP strategy, students can use the GRASP graphic organizer (page 162) to write their summaries independently.

Differentiation

Remind ELLs and students reading and writing below grade level to use the text as reference. ELLs might also benefit from having a sheet with the key points that the students can use in their summary statements. Gifted students can complete this activity independently from the beginning.

Summary-Writing Strategies for Social Studies *(cont.)*

Guided Reading and Summarizing Procedure *(cont.)*

Grades 3–5 Example

Details Remembered from Reading	Additions/Corrections
–life in Southern states was very different from Northeast –South did not have as many cities –South had mostly farms and plantations –differences created different needs –South grew cotton on the plantations (greater need for workers) –slavery supported plantations –slave families were separated at slave auctions	–growing cotton required a lot of workers, even after cotton gin –slaves made up the large number of workers needed –slaves had difficult life on the plantations –slaves could be bought and sold –most slaves who tried to escape were hurt and beaten but not killed, slave owners needed slaves to do their work

Main Ideas in Reading
–The South had a different living style than the North. –Slaves were used as workers on large plantations. –Cotton was a profitable crop.

Summary-Writing Strategies for Social Studies *(cont.)*

Guided Reading and Summarizing Procedure *(cont.)*

Grades 6–8 Example

Details Remembered from Reading	Additions/Corrections
–Underground Railroad was not an actual railroad –Underground Railroad was a network of people that helped slaves hide as they traveled and escaped to Northern states –Harriet Tubman a "conductor" on the Underground Railroad –Tubman helped hundreds of slaves escape –songs helped slaves survive slavery and the poor conditions and shared messages of how to escape slavery –slave hunters searched for slaves –many slaves voluntarily returned home and were punished severely	–Some states were considered slave states while others were free states. –Slavery was not allowed in the free states. –Slaves were trying to travel north to the free states and into Canada.

Main Ideas in Reading
–Slavery was a big part of American history. –Slaves tried to run away on the Underground Railroad. –There were both free and slave states in the United States during this time.

Name: _____

Guided Reading and Summarizing Procedure

Directions: Use this chart to help you summarize the main ideas of a reading passage. After the first reading, write the details you remember in the upper left-hand box. After the second reading, write any additions or corrections to your original information. Finally, synthesize the information into a few main ideas, and write them in the bottom box.

Details Remembered from Reading	Additions/Corrections

Main Ideas in Reading

Applying Knowledge in Social Studies

What Does the Research Say?

Research is showing that writing-to-learn activities or expressive writing activities have a place in the social studies curriculum. This is not to say that the formal types of writing originally found in the social studies classroom should be excluded. Transactional writing, as Britton, et al (1975) calls it, is the kind of writing that has a specific purpose. There is the intent to produce something. There is a specific audience and the writer is responsible for what he or she says. Most transactional writing ends up as a finished product and is often called *product writing*. There is emphasis on what the final product will look like. This type of writing is more formal and is the most common form of writing in the social studies classroom. Examples of product writing include historical fiction pieces, biographies, essays, and research reports, as well as responses to test questions.

Students should be taught how to complete product writing. Students should have models and examples to follow. Teachers should be expected to teach students how to write formal social studies pieces (Sorenson 1989; Winchester 1987; Hamilton-Wieler 1988). With this form of writing, the student is accountable for spelling, grammar, and punctuation decisions. Writing mechanics and organization are as much a part of the grade as the content will be. Strategies on how to incorporate examples of social studies product writing into the classroom are explained in this section of the book.

Much nonfiction reading and writing readily lends itself to the application of knowledge. It is something we do quite naturally in many situations (Koedinger and Tabachneck 1994). Writing-to-apply activities provide students with the opportunity to write about social studies concepts using established formats such as research reports, essays, and lab reports. Writing for an audience requires understanding of subject, organization, and complex cognitive thought. Writing-to-apply activities encourage critical thinking skills in formal settings. These same skills can transfer to writing that will be done throughout life in the workplace and elsewhere.

The more students write, the more familiar and the more comfortable they will become. Students need instruction, direction, experience, and motivation to write. Incorporating transactional or product writing in the social studies class allows students to develop a knowledge of the writing process and each phase. It also allows students to weave together the language of social studies into everyday language and conversation. Finally, product writing exposes students to writing for an audience and writing for a variety of purposes.

Writing Applications for Social Studies

Summary–Writing Microtheme

Background Information

The Microthemes strategy introduced by John C. Bean (1996) enables students to write what they know about a specific theme. In essence, the microtheme is a condensed version of a research report or essay, written on one side of a 5" x 8" index card. This strategy reveals what the student does or does not know about a specific social studies subject. It provides an opportunity for students to write informally using clear and accurate information for an intended audience. With this microtheme, students determine which details to eliminate and which to condense. Ideally, this application activity would follow practice with GIST, Key Words, or Guided Reading and Summarizing Procedures so that students are well prepared to create their own summaries independently. The focus of the Summary-Writing Microtheme is to improve students' comprehension and summarizing abilities.

Grade Levels/Standards Addressed

Grades 3–5 (Standard 1.11)
Grades 6–8 (Standard 1.12)

Genres

Summary

Stages of Writing Process

Prewrite, Draft, Revise, Edit, Publish

Activity

Select a piece of text that is well suited for summary writing. Tell students that they will write a short summary about the text. Display a sample Summary-Writing Microtheme on the board or overhead and discuss the organization (main ideas and details), tone (direct), language (content vocabulary), and other features (transition words). Set clear expectations for students, so they will be successful. Next, model writing a Summary-Writing Microtheme, using a prewriting strategy, drafting, revising, editing, and publishing. This is probably best done over several days or class periods. Distribute copies of the Summary-Writing Microtheme planning sheet (page 165) to get students started on the writing process.

Differentiation

If appropriate, allow ELLs to use pictures or other visual representations in their microthemes. Remind these students to focus on summarizing the text in an organized manner. Consider providing them with summary frames or sentence stems if these will help ELLs better communicate the information. Do not hold ELLs accountable for spelling and writing conventions as much as for content. Encourage gifted students to write a report after completing the microtheme. Or have them write a Summary-Writing Microtheme on two different texts about the same topic then compare and contrast the information. Provide small-group instruction for students reading and writing below grade level at each stage of the writing process. These students may need support to organize their information in a systematic manner and to use the prewriting work to create a draft. Allow additional time for these students to accomplish the assignment.

Name: _____

Summary-Writing Microtheme

Directions: Use this prewriting planner to organize your Summary-Writing Microtheme.

Main Idea

_____

_____

Detail

_____

_____

Detail

_____

_____

Detail

_____

_____

Closing Statement

_____

_____

Reminders:
- Refer back to the text to identify the main idea.
- Make sure the details support or are related to the main idea.
- Use this outline to write your draft.
- Add transition words (most importantly, for example, etc.).

Writing Applications for Social Studies *(cont.)*

Thesis–Support Microtheme

Background Information

With this microtheme, the student takes a stand on an assigned scientific issue. After conducting some research on the issue or reviewing notes from class, students are ready to write the Thesis-Support Microtheme. The main stance or thesis statement by the student should include three main supportive statements.

Grade Levels/Standards Addressed

Grades 3–5 (Standard 1.7)
Grades 6–8 (Standard 1.6)

Genres

Expository

Stages of Writing Process

Prewrite, Draft, Revise, Edit, Publish

Activity

Identify an issue in social studies that is well suited for thesis writing. Tell students that they will write a thesis with supporting statements to communicate their position on the issue. Display a sample Thesis-Support Microtheme on the board or overhead and discuss the organization (main ideas and details), tone (direct and persuasive), language (content-specific vocabulary and persuasive language), and other features (transition words). Set clear expectations, so students will understand how to be successful. Next, model writing your own Thesis-Support Microtheme: use a prewriting strategy, draft, revise, edit, and publish.

Distribute copies of the Thesis-Support Microtheme planning sheet (page 167) to get students started on the writing process. Although this is a short writing application activity, consider modeling over several days or class periods so students are clear on how to create an effective microtheme.

Differentiation

If appropriate, allow ELLs to use pictures or other visual representations in their microthemes. Remind these students to focus on the organization of the microtheme—a clear stance and three supporting statements. Consider providing them with a list of persuasive language to incorporate into their writing. Do not hold ELLs accountable for spelling and writing conventions as much as for content. Challenge gifted students to include more supporting statements in their Thesis-Support Microtheme. Or, encourage them to develop two Thesis-Support Microthemes—one to support their original thesis and one to support an opposing viewpoint. Provide small-group instruction for students reading and writing below grade level at each stage of the writing process. These students may need support to organize their information in a systematic manner and to use the prewriting work to create a draft. Allow additional time for these students to accomplish the assignment.

Name: _____

Thesis-Support Microtheme

Directions: Use this prewriting planner to organize your Thesis-Support Microtheme.

Thesis Statement/Main Stance

_____

_____

Supporting Information

_____

_____

Supporting Information

_____

_____

Supporting Information

_____

_____

Closing Statement

_____

_____

Reminders:

- Take a clear stance in your first statement.
- Make sure the details support or are related to your thesis.
- Use this outline to write your draft.
- Add transition words (most importantly, for example, etc.).

Writing Applications for Social Studies *(cont.)*

Data-Provided Microtheme

Background Information

The Data-Provided Microtheme is a diagram, table, or chart drawn by the students to explain a process. This graphic should include details and descriptions using color, if necessary. Brief descriptions and details should be thorough and condensed.

Grade Levels/Standards Addressed

Grades 3–5 (Standard 4.8)
Grades 6–8 (Standard 4.5)

Genres

Expository

Stages of Writing Process

Prewrite, Draft, Revise, Edit, Publish

Activity

Select a piece of text that is well suited to visual representations. Tell students that they will create a diagram, table, or chart to communicate the important information in the text. Display a sample Data-Provided Microtheme on the board or overhead and discuss its features: title, visual representation (diagram, table, or chart), labels (for rows, columns, or diagrams), illustrations (when appropriate), and use of color. Set clear expectations for students, so they will be successful. Next, model creating a Data-Support Microtheme, using a prewriting strategy, drafting, revising, editing, and publishing. Then distribute copies of the Data-Provided Microtheme planning sheet (page 169) to help students begin the writing process. Although this is a short writing application activity, consider modeling over several days or class periods so students are clear on how to create an effective microtheme.

Differentiation

With adequate teacher modeling, ELLs should be very successful with this microtheme. Challenge gifted students to include more details in their diagrams and more complex categories in the charts and tables. Or, encourage them to present their microtheme to the class and explain how they determined the appropriate titles, representation, and labels. Meet with students reading and writing below grade level during the prewriting phase to make sure they are choosing an appropriate visual representation and organizing the information correctly. Allow additional time for these students to accomplish the assignment.

Name: _____

Data-Provided Microtheme

Directions: Use this prewriting planner to organize your Data-Provided Microtheme.

Reminders:

- Refer back to the text to gather information, words, or data.
- Choose a visual presentation—chart, graph, diagram, table, graphic organizer, etc.—that will best represent the information.
- Give your Data-Provided Microtheme a title.
- Label rows, columns, headings, etc.
- Use color where appropriate.

Writing Applications for Social Studies *(cont.)*

Quandary-Posing Microtheme

Background Information

The Quandary-Posing Microtheme poses a social studies-related problem as presented by the student. The student must incorporate principals that can be applied in solving the problem. The focus is to be creative and accurate in solving the problem.

Grade Levels/Standards Addressed

Grades 3–5 (Standard 1.7)
Grades 6–8 (Standard 1.6, 1.11)

Genres

Expository

Stages of Writing Process

Prewrite, Draft, Revise, Edit, Publish

Activity

Select a social studies topic that is well suited to identifying problems and creating solutions. Tell students that they will identify a problem and develop a solution. Display a sample Quandary-Posing Microtheme on the board or overhead and discuss its features: a question about the social studies topic, a proposed solution, and the reasons why that solution is appropriate. Set clear expectations for students, so they will be successful. Next, model creating a Quandary-Posing Microtheme, using a prewriting strategy, drafting, revising, editing, and publishing.

Then distribute copies of the Quandary-Posing planning sheet (page 171) to help students begin the writing process. Although this is a short writing application activity, be sure to model over several days or class periods so students are clear on how to create an effective microtheme.

Differentiation

Make sure that ELLs clearly understand the terms *problem* and *solution*. Explicitly model for ELLs how to organize this microtheme and provide them with sentence frames to use in their writing. Challenge gifted students to present and describe multiple solutions to their problems. Meet with students reading and writing below grade level during the prewriting phase to make sure their solutions address the problem. This is a good opportunity for discussing possible solutions and their outcomes. Allow additional time for these students to accomplish the assignment.

Name: _____

Quandary-Posing Microtheme

Directions: Use this prewriting planner to organize your Quandary-Posing Microtheme.

Problem

_____

_____

_____

Possible Solution

_____

_____

_____

Why it Will Work

_____

_____

_____

Closing Statement

_____

_____

_____

> **Reminders:**
> - Clearly identify and describe the problem.
> - Make sure the solution will solve the problem.
> - Explain why your solution will be effective.
> - Add cause-and-effect words (as a result, because, due to, etc.)

Writing Applications for Social Studies *(cont.)*

RAFT Assignment

Background Information

RAFT stands for Role, Audience, Format, and Topic, the key ingredients of writing assignments (Santa, Havens, and Harrison 1996). This particular writing assignment alters the usual assignment in which students write a formal essay or report. With this activity, teachers can encourage creative application of social studies content knowledge. Writers may be asked to write from the point of view of a bill (role) speaking to a group of senators (audience) in a speech (format) about the process of the bill becoming a law (topic).

Grade Levels/Standards Addressed

Grades 1–2 (Standard 1.7–1.8)
Grades 3–5 (Standard 1.5, 1.6)
Grades 6–8 (Standard 1.5)

Genres

Expository, Summary, Narrative, Persuasive

Stages of Writing Process

Prewrite, Draft, Edit, Revise, Publish

Activity

Prepare the RAFT Assignment sheet by filling in the RAFT components. Distribute copies of the sheet to students, then hold a brainstorming session to share ideas on how to address each area in the writing. Provide plenty of time for students to collaborate and get excited about the assignment. Model writing your own RAFT assignment, showing each step of the writing process before asking students to work on their own. If needed, provide students with copies of a genre-specific graphic organizer (see pages 108–139) during the prewriting phase. Consider incorporating other authoring strategies throughout the writing process, such as Author's Chair (pages 146–148).

Variation

Primary grade teachers may want to create a RAFT piece as a whole class, using the shared writing process on a large piece of chart paper. Provide a beginning for the writing piece, then ask students to contribute ideas to continue the story. Invite various students to come up and write each sentence on the chart until the story is complete. If grade level teams are working on the RAFT assignment, teachers may rotate the complete stories, so that students can see the creative ideas of the other classes.

Differentiation

Allow ELLs to draw pictures in a story map to get them started. Modify the writing expectations to meet their individual levels. Students who are reading and writing below grade level may need more explicit instruction in the chosen genre, so consider meeting with these students in small groups to preteach the features of the genre before beginning writing. Also provide graphic organizers to help them stay organized. Gifted students may be thrilled with the freedom of the assignment. They should be able to work independently, but challenge them appropriately to develop their writing skills further.

Name: _____

RAFT Assignment

Directions: Use this prewriting planner to organize your RAFT Assignment.

Role: _____

Audience: _____

Form: _____

Topic: _____

Reminders:

· Think carefully about your role and your point of view.

· Consider how to best communicate to your audience.

· Use the traits of the writing form. You may wish to create a graphic organizer specific to that genre: for example, a letter, poem, explanation, or story.

· Stay focused on your topic.

Writing Applications for Social Studies *(cont.)*

Business Letter

Background Information

Writing a business letter is another expressive writing strategy that provides students with the opportunity to persuade others on a social studies topic. Send the business letters out and read and post replies as they come into the classroom.

Grade Levels/Standards Addressed

Grades 1–2 (Standard 1.7)
Grades 3–5 (Standard 1.12)
Grades 6–8 (Standard 1.13)

Genres

Narrative, Persuasive

Stages of Writing Process

Prewrite, Draft, Revise, Edit, Publish

Activity

Review the following questions with the students:

- What is the purpose of a business letter?
- Can you think of an example of a business letter that contains a social studies topic?
- What key features of a business letter should be included?
- What are some tips for writing a business letter relating to a social studies topic?

Divide the class into groups of three or four. Have each group make a list of ideas for business letters with a social studies theme.

Examples may include the following:

- Write a letter to the editor about a public school issue.
- Write a letter to a government worker or public official asking about their job.
- Write a letter to the editor stating an opinion on whether or not a local ordinance should be passed.
- Write a letter to the mayor to ask for support on a problem in your neighborhood.
- Write a letter to your city's public information office asking about your city's history.

Allow time for students to share their responses with the class. Call on students to share examples of business letters with a social studies theme. Distribute copies of the Business Letter graphic organizer (page 175), and allow students to write a business letter on a social studies topic.

Differentiation

Encourage ELLs to write the letter independently and pair them with a partner for editing and revising. Pair them with students who are comfortable with writing formally. Encourage gifted students to write letters on a controversial social studies topic to a member of Congress or a local politician. This will require the student to present an argument and think through the problem to suggest solutions. Students who are reading and writing below grade level will benefit from working with a partner to write the letter.

Name: _____

Business Letter

_____

_____
_____
_____

_____
_____
_____

To Whom It May Concern: (or) Dear _____:

_____
_____
_____
_____

_____
_____
_____
_____

_____
_____
_____

_____,

_____

Writing Applications for Social Studies *(cont.)*

Friendly Letter

Background Information

Writing a friendly letter is another expressive writing strategy that provides students with the opportunity to persuade others on a social studies topic. Send friendly letters out and read and post replies as they arrive.

Grade Levels/Standards Addressed

Grades 1–2 (Standard 1.7)
Grades 3–5 (Standard 1.12)
Grades 6–8 (Standard 1.13)

Genres

Narrative, Persuasive

Stages of Writing Process

Prewrite, Draft, Revise, Edit, Publish

Activity

Review the following questions with the students:

- What is the purpose of a friendly letter?

- Can you think of an example of a friendly letter that contains a social studies topic?

- What key features of a friendly letter should be included?

- What are some tips for writing a friendly letter relating to a social studies topic?

Divide the class into groups of three or four. Have each group make a list of examples of a friendly letter with a social studies theme. Examples may include the following:

- Letter to a friend explaining a social studies experiment that the student enjoyed.

- Letter to a family member explaining what has been learned in social studies.

- Letter to a friend encouraging him or her to support a bill on a social studies-related topic.

Allow time for students to share their responses with the class. Call on students to share examples of friendly letters with a social studies theme. Distribute copies of the Friendly Letter planning sheet (page 177), and allow students to write a friendly letter of their own on a social studies topic.

Differentiation

Encourage ELLs to write letters independently and pair them with partners for editing and revising. Pair them with students who are comfortable with writing formally. Encourage gifted students to write about a more complex topic, or challenge them to include more advanced vocabulary and complex sentence structures. Students who are reading and writing below grade level will benefit from working with a partner to write the letter.

Name: _____

Friendly Letter

_____

Dear _____,

_____

_____

_____

_____

_____

_____

_____

_____

_____,

_____

Writing Applications for Social Studies *(cont.)*

Historical Biography

Background Information

The historical biography is an opportunity for students to develop historical empathy and learn more in-depth information about a historical time period by conducting research about a key figure of the period. Students use research skills, note-taking strategies, writing strategies, and summary skills.

Grade Levels/Standards Addressed

Grades 1–2 (Standard 1.7)
Grades 3–5 (Standard 1.7)
Grades 6–8 (Standard 1.6)

Genres

Expository

Stages of Writing Process

Prewrite, Draft, Revise, Edit, Publish

Activity

Discuss historical biographies with students and review each section in detail. Take time to model each step of the writing process as you write your own historical biography. Students will benefit from hearing the "thinking aloud."

1. **Title**—What title would capture your readers' attention? Considering modeling a play on words, the use of alliteration, or a question.

2. **Introduction**—Why did you choose to write about this person? Do you have a special interest in their accomplishments or a connection with their life story? Students can express their personal feelings in this section.

3. **Childhood**—When and where was the person born? What did you learn about his or her family? What was difficult or unique about the person's childhood experience? Students may be particularly interested in this information because they can relate to it.

4. **Achievements**—What is this person known for? What obstacles did they overcome to meet their goals? What lasting effects did those accomplishments have on their community, the country, or the world? The focus of these paragraphs may differ depending on the subject and their accomplishments.

5. **Conclusion**—Here, students summarize the achievements of their subject. Students also explain what they learned from writing the biography and how they can apply this learning to their own lives.

Differentiation

If appropriate, allow ELLs to draw and label pictures for each section. Then, working in small groups, use sentence frames (i.e. Abraham Lincoln was born in _____.) to help these students complete their biographies. ELLs and students reading and writing below grade level will benefit from frequent writing conferences for feedback and additional scaffolding. Challenge gifted students to complement their biographies with a unique addition, such as a hand-drawn map of the person's hometown, a reinactment of a famous speech, or a song about the person's life.

Name: _____

Historical Biography

Title: How can you capture your readers' attention? What would make an interesting title?

_____

_____

Introduction: Why did you choose to study this historical figure?

_____

_____

Childhood: When and where was this person born? Tell about his or her childhood experience.

_____

_____

Achievement #1: Provide details about why this was important or what obstacles were overcome.

_____

_____

_____

Achievement #2: Provide details about why this was important or what obstacles were overcome.

_____

_____

_____

Conclusion: Explain what you learned from this research. How will you apply it to your own life?

_____

_____

_____

Writing Applications for Social Studies *(cont.)*

Newspaper Article

Background Information

Writing a newspaper article on a social studies-related theme is another way for students to use social studies in everyday life. The article usually answers the *who, what, where, when, why,* and *how* questions.

Activity

Divide the class into groups of three or four and give each group a newspaper or age-appropriate periodical. Ask groups to locate and cut out an article about a social studies topic. Write the following list on the board, and discuss the elements of a newspaper article.

A newspaper article has . . .

- **headline**—This is a short, concise phrase that explains the main point of the article.

- **byline**—This is the name of the person who wrote the newspaper article.

- **dateline**—This lists the month, day, and year the article was written.

- **illustration**—An illustration is optional to a newspaper article. It can help bring the point of the story home to the reader.

- **paragraph 1**—This should answer the who, what, when, and where questions.

- **paragraph 2**—This should answer the how and why questions. Answering how and why takes the reader to the next step.

- **last paragraph**—This is usually a conclusion, summary, or list of future prospects.

Explain that a newspaper article addresses the five W's—*who, what, where, when,* and *why*—and anticipates and answers readers' questions. A newspaper article can address difficult issues and questions related to social studies or it can document a new trend in social studies. Use page 181 to analyze the article and then ask students to write a newspaper article on a social studies topic.

Differentiation

Make sure ELLs clearly understand the social studies topic, through review, discussion, use of graphic organizers, etc., before beginning to write. Then provide resource books for them during the writing process so that they look up words. Take extra time to make sure all of the words and phrases on the board are clearly defined and understood by students reading and writing below grade level. Use visuals whenever possible. Both ELLs and students reading and writing below grade level will benefit from working in mixed-ability groups. Have gifted students work in teams to design a social studies newspaper dedicated to the social studies topics being studied in class.

Name: _____

Newspaper Article

Directions: Read the newspaper article carefully, and then answer the questions below.

Who

Who is the article about? _____

Who would be interested in reading it? _____

Who is the audience? _____

What

What is the purpose of the article? _____

What is the main idea of the article? How does it relate to social studies?

_____

What is the author's desired result? _____

When

When does the event in the story take place? _____

When was the story written? _____

Where

Where does the news story take place? _____

Where is the newspaper circulated? _____

Why

Why was this printed in the newspaper instead of a book or other reference?

_____

Why did the events in the news story happen? _____

Why did the author write the article? What can be learned about social studies as a result of this article? _____

Writing Applications for Social Studies *(cont.)*

Historical Fiction

Background Information

Historical fiction is a great tool for students to weave social studies knowledge into everyday life. In order for a piece of historical fiction to be believable, it must contain some convincing social studies information. Look for opportunities throughout the social studies lessons to point out social studies problems that could be incorporated into a story.

Grade Levels/Standards Addressed

Grades 1–2 (Standard 1.7)
Grades 3–5 (Standard 1.8)
Grades 6–8 (Standard 1.7)

Genres

Narrative

Stages of Writing Process

Prewrite, Draft, Revise, Edit, Publish

Activity

Read a chapter of an historical fiction piece. Identify with the class the social studies-related problem and possible solutions. Discuss the main elements of a story:

- setting
- characters
- problem
- solution

Explain that a story has a beginning, middle, and an end. The beginning usually describes the setting and introduces the characters. The reader learns more about the characters and the problem in the middle of the story. The ending tells the solution to the problem. Point out that social studies facts and details need to be woven into the story and the plot. Work together as a class to write a story outline. Record student ideas on the board or overhead.

First, discuss the characters. Which characters should be in the story? Remember to limit the number of characters. Too many characters can lead to confusion. Brainstorm with students some settings and problems for their stories. Spend time researching the social studies topic, so students have a clear understanding of the topic and how it could be an issue in everyday life. Write each sentence as a class. Call on one student at a time to add to the story.

Once the story is written, read it to the class. Analyze how well the social studies elements were handled. Identify any changes or additions that need to be made. Then have students use the Historical Fiction outline (page 183) to write their own piece of historical fiction.

Differentiation

Give ELLs resources such as dual-language dictionaries, picture books, and encyclopedias at their reading level. Hold frequent conferences with ELLs and students reading and writing below grade level throughout the writing process to provide modeling, feedback, and scaffolding. Challenge gifted students to include richer vocabulary, more dynamic language, and more complex sentence structures. Encourage gifted students to conduct research about the social studies content prior to writing the story.

Name: _____

Historical Fiction

Directions: Use this story map to help you plan your historical fiction story. Follow the arrows to the next step.

Setting (Where and when does the story takes place?)

Characters (Who or what are the people, places, or things in the story?)

Conflict/Problem (What is the social studies-related problem?)

Action/Events (What are the attempts to solve the problem?)

Solution (How does the story end?)

Writing Applications for Social Studies *(cont.)*

Social Studies Research Report

Background Information

A common writing assignment in the social studies classroom is the research report in which students are expected to research a social studies concept and write about their findings.

Grade Levels/Standards Addressed

Grades 3–5 (Standard 4.8)
Grades 6–8 (Standard 4.6)

Genres

Expository

Stages of Writing Process

Prewrite, Draft, Revise, Edit, Publish

Activity

Provide a variety of resources for students on various social studies topics. Allow time for students to peruse the materials and choose a topic of interest that they would like to research. You may also choose to assign a research topic to students based on your available resources. Demonstrate how to access online resources or how to use other resources that may be available outside of school, such as magazines, newspaper articles, television specials, etc.

Once students have gathered basic information, they are ready to start the research process. Instruct them to write the main idea of their research report. Encourage students to discuss their topic with a partner. Once you have approved the topic, students can begin thoroughly researching it. Use the Social Studies Research Report planner (page 185) to help students organize their information. The outline lists the main topic and supporting ideas.

Allow plenty of time for students to draft, revise, and edit their reports. Consider using the Author's Chair strategy (see pages 146–148) at this stage of the writing process. Group participants can ask questions, anticipate problems, or point out details that have been left out.

Conference individually with students when they have completed the rough draft of their research report. Students can use the tips in the Writing Process section of this book to assist in the editing of these reports. Show students how to cite the resources they used for the report.

Differentiation

Provide ELLs with visuals and extended review on research material to help them gain a clear understanding of the information. Challenge gifted students to research and write about a more complex topic. Require them to cite resources. Hold frequent writing conferences with ELLs and students reading and writing below grade level to model, provide feedback, and scaffold the writing process. Also, conduct mini-lessons to preteach the next step of the writing process.

Name: _____

Social Studies Research Report

Directions: Use this prewriting planner to help you organize your Social Studies Research Report.

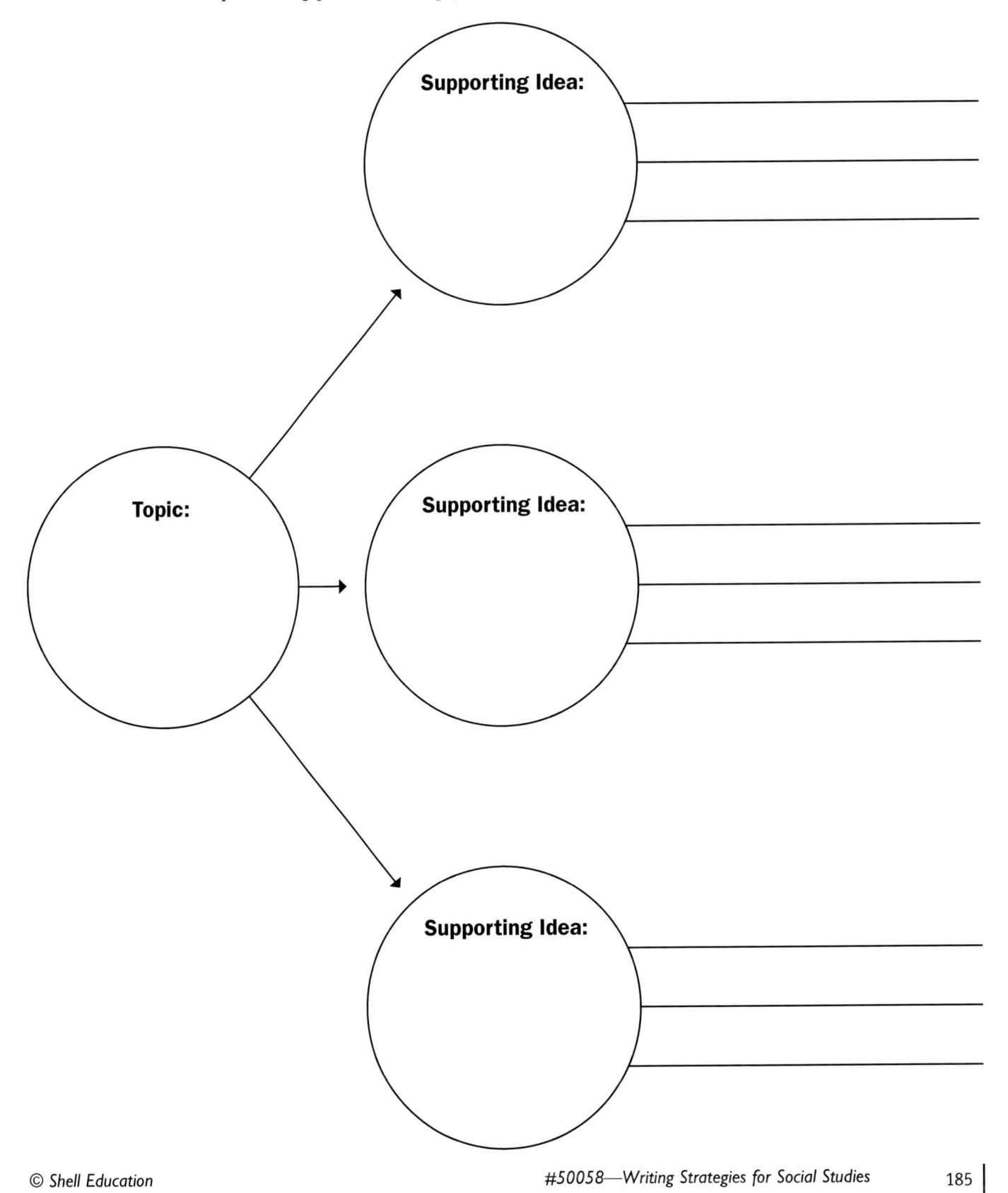

Assessing Writing in Social Studies

Role of Assessment of Writing in the Social Studies Classroom

The role of assessment of writing in social studies class has been another reason social studies teachers avoid writing (Gahn 1989). However, not all writing assignments or activities in social studies need to be graded. Writing-to-learn assignments seldom need to be graded. These experiences are to provide opportunities for students to express themselves and what they are learning. The concern for how to grade more formal writing assignments can be alleviated with rubrics and checklists. These two methods can be effective and meaningful ways to assess more formal types of writing in social studies. Writing assessments will be described and discussed in detail in the last section of this book.

Authentic Assessment of Writing

Views of teaching and learning have changed to include the concept of constructivism—the belief that learners actively and dynamically construct the information they are learning about the world. The learner is not an "empty cup," to be filled with knowledge and information. Constructivism holds a view that learning includes and incorporates a dynamic and active mental process (e.g. Jones et al. 1987; Marzano, Pickering, and McTighe 1993; Resnick and Klopfer 1989). Students learn through interactive and integrative experiences in the classroom; the more a student actively listens, speaks, reads, writes, and thinks, the easier the learning and retention of knowledge will be.

There are a variety of ways to construct knowledge and learn (Pressley and Associates 1990; Weinstein and Mayer 1986), but one of the key ways to help learning occur is to have students write.

Although many teachers agree with the notion of interactive learning, they feel inadequate when grading or assessing this type of learning. For example, how does a teacher grade writing in social studies? How does a teacher assign a grade to something that is not formal writing? How does the teacher assess the learning of social studies skills and concepts through writing? These concerns are valid. Assessment of this type of writing must validate learning, and it must acknowledge the social studies standards and objectives as well. Authentic assessment reflects back on the meaningful instruction and learning process. There are many different types of authentic assessment of writing done in the classroom (Feuer and Fulton 1993). There is room for authentic assessment in the social studies classroom too!

Incorporating authentic assessment in the social studies classroom requires little time, effort, or experience. It is not uncommon for a social studies teacher to feel uncomfortable grading students' writing, but they may realize that they are already using some types of authentic assessment in their classroom. The types of authentic assessments that lend themselves to writing in the social studies classroom include holistic assessment, primary trait assessment, and analytic scoring (Cohen 1994; Herman, Aschbacher, and Winters 1992). Examples of these are included in the following pages.

Self-assessment and peer assessments provide opportunities for students to reflect on their own writing abilities as well as their social studies understanding. Peer assessment also provides other examples of writing for students to read and compare and contrast with their own writing and understanding.

Strategies for Assessing Writing in Social Studies

Holistic Assessment

Background Information

Holistic Assessment evaluates the overall picture of the writing as opposed to the individual writing components. This assessment uses a list of criteria that are analyzed to produce one score, on a scale of 1–6. The criteria, which address both social studies objectives and writing skills, are determined prior to the assignment and the student is informed of the criteria before writing takes place. The criteria can be adapted to meet students' needs and the objectives of the assignment. The four main criteria are as follows:

- Idea Development/Organization—Does the student communicate a central idea or purpose? Has this idea been supported throughout the piece and is there a conclusion?

- Fluency/Structure—Does the student use correct grammar (verb endings, verb tenses, pronouns, etc.) and syntax in the writing?

- Word Choice—Does the student incorporate a variety of words and content-specific terms?

- Mechanics—Does the student use correct spelling, capitalization, and punctuation?

Grade Levels/Standards Addressed

Grades 1–2 (Standard 1.4)
Grades 3–5 (Standard 1.4)
Grades 6–8 (Standard 1.4)

Genres

Expository, Summary, Narrative, Persuasive

Stages of Writing Process

Reflection

Activity

Prior to beginning a writing assignment, distribute copies of the Holistic Assessment (page 188) and review and discuss it. (Please note that this rubric can be altered to fit the needs of the writing assignment and the age of the students.) Be sure that they are clear on the expectations of the writing assignment and on how they will be assessed prior to beginning the writing. You may also choose to include students in creating the criteria. After students complete the writing, pair each student with a partner to exchange the writing and provide suggestions, comments, and feedback. Then collect students' writing and use the rubric to rate each piece with a score from 1–6.

Differentiation

Adapt the rubric to meet the needs of ELLs and their abilities. They may not be expected to meet the grade-level expectations in grammar and mechanics, for example. Challenge gifted students to create their own criteria and rubric. Help students who read and write below grade level use the rubric throughout the writing process to meet the expectations.

Name: _____

Holistic Assessment

Title: _____ **Topic:** _____

Level 6 Writing conveys clear meaning and ideas.	
–organizes the piece with multi-paragraphs, and develops ideas and a conclusion	
–incorporates smooth transitions	
–incorporates necessary social studies concepts and ideas	
–uses a variety of vocabulary, including social studies vocabulary and terms	
–writing has few or no grammatical or mechanical errors	

Level 5 Writing conveys meaning and ideas.	
–organizes the piece with multi-paragraphs, though some portions may not be fully developed	
–incorporates some smooth transitions	
–incorporates some social studies concepts and ideas	
–uses some social studies vocabulary and terms	
–writing has some grammatical or mechanical errors	

Level 4 Writing expresses an idea most of the time.	
–develops a cohesive paragraph	
–uses a variety of sentence structures with few transitions	
–selects some social studies vocabulary and terms	
–writing has some grammatical or mechanical errors	

Level 3 Begins to write about an idea but fails to support it.	
–sometimes develops a cohesive paragraph	
–uses complete sentences	
–incorporates few social studies vocabulary and terms	
–writing has many grammatical or mechanical errors	

Level 2 Attempts to write about an idea.	
–there are no cohesive paragraphs	
–uses complete sentences sometimes	
–lack of social studies vocabulary and terms incorporated in writing	
–writing has multiple grammatical or mechanical errors	

Level 1 There is no common theme or idea.	
–sentences are written but incomplete	
–uses sentences with few transitions	
–social studies vocabulary and terms are not used	
–writing has too many grammatical or mechanical errors	

Strategies for Assessing Writing in Social Studies *(cont.)*

Analytic Assessment

Background Information

With analytic assessment, each component of the writing is analyzed independently of the others and given its own score. The writing assignment is given several scores, each representing the different components. The teacher may also choose to weigh one component more heavily than another to add emphasis. Analytic assessment not only allows the teacher to provide specific feedback to students, but it also helps the teacher target certain areas in planning, instruction, and assessment (Perkins 1983).

Grade Levels/Standards Addressed

Grades 1–2 (Standard 1.4)
Grades 3–5 (Standard 1.4)
Grades 6–8 (Standard 1.4)

Genres

Expository, Summary, Narrative, Persuasive

Stages of Writing Process

Reflection

Activity

Create with students a rubric that scores each component of the writing assignment. The writing components may include composition, mechanics, sentence formation, social studies content, and usage. Determine if one component of the rubric should receive more emphasis than another. Determine the number of points scored for each component. Review the Analytic Assessment (page 190) with students prior to giving instructions on the writing assignment. Be sure students understand how they will be graded. Show models of writing samples. Allow time for students to complete the writing assignment and then compare it to the designated rubric. Students can then edit and make changes as they deem necessary. Make copies of the analytic assessment rubric and use it to score the students' writing assignments.

Differentiation

Work independently with ELLs to create a rubric that meets their specific needs to ensure a greater chance of success. If desired, include a component of writing English as part of the rubric. Encourage gifted students to create their own rubrics, score their writing assignments, and compare them with the scores you determined for the writing. You may also weigh certain components more heavily to challenge gifted students. If appropriate, adapt rubrics for students who are reading and writing below grade level to address their individual needs.

Name: _____

Analytic Assessment

Title: _____ **Date:** _____

Topic: _____

Skill	Excellent (3 points)	Satisfactory (2 points)	Needs Improvement (1 point)
Stays on topic			
Shows a clear purpose (topic sentence)			
Includes supporting details with specific examples			
Has sequential and/or logical development			
Includes a main idea paragraph			
Clearly presents social studies concepts			
Expresses ideas clearly			
Uses complete sentences			
Uses varied sentence types and structures			
Uses social studies words correctly			
Uses correct spelling			

Comments: _____

_____

_____

Strategies for Assessing Writing in Social Studies (cont.)

Primary Trait Assessment

Background Information

Primary Trait Assessment is a way for the teacher to focus on one specific skill or trait. The teacher determines the skill, trait, or feature that will be analyzed and assessed in a piece of writing. The trait can be writing-based or social studies-based depending on the intent of the lesson. In primary trait writing, only the focus or primary trait is scored. The other traits and elements are ignored.

A benefit to using the Primary Trait Assessment is that students may feel more at ease with the primary trait focus because they can focus on one area. Teachers too can focus on specific areas of concern. The Primary Trait Assessment also allows the teacher to focus specifically on the social studies skill or concept while ignoring the mechanics and composition areas of writing.

Grade Levels/Standards Addressed

Grades 1–2 (Standard 1.4)
Grades 3–5 (Standard 1.4)
Grades 6–8 (Standard 1.4)

Genres

Expository, Summary, Narrative, Persuasive

Stages of Writing Process

Reflection

Activity

Determine the writing assignment to be used for the primary trait assessment rubric for scoring. Select the specific trait or skill that you would like students to focus on during the writing assignment. Display a copy of the Primary Trait Assessment (page 192) for students to see before they begin writing. Tell students the primary trait that is the focus for this writing assignment. Explain that the other areas of writing will be ignored for assessment purposes. Allow time for students to draft and edit their writing before submitting it for assessment. If desired, pair students with partners to edit one another's writing. When using the Primary Trait Assessment rubric, be sure to give specific feedback on how students can improve in this primary trait. Use this rubric the next time students write so that you can look for progress on the primary trait.

Differentiation

Select a primary trait for ELLs to fit their specific language needs. Challenge gifted students by selecting a primary trait that is not a clear strength, and have gifted students decide how to improve their area of focus. Give specific feedback to students reading and writing below grade level on what they need to improve and encourage them to revise and edit their work. Design a specific primary trait focus that will meet their individual needs.

Name: _____

Primary Trait Assessment

Title: _____ **Date:** _____

Topic: _____

Select the primary trait for focus and use the following rubric (with adjustments, if needed) to assess students' writing. Leave specific feedback.

5 The student demonstrates desired skills throughout the text.

4 Most of the time, the student demonstrates desired skills in the text.

3 Occasionally, the student demonstrates desired skills in the text.

2 Seldom does the student demonstrate desired skills in the text.

1 The student is not using desired skills in the text.

_____ **Content:**
The writer presents a main point and uses a clear organizational structure. The writer presents information logically. The writer anticipates and addresses the concerns and questions of the reader. The writer cites sources of information whenever necessary. The writer uses books and other resources to gather information. The writer conveys an intended purpose in writing. The writer understands and portrays the concepts of social studies in a meaningful way.
Comments: _____
_____ **Writing Conventions:**
The writer has taken time and effort to ensure the writing does not have spelling errors. Each sentence begins with a capital and ends with the correct punctuation. The writing contains clear transitions to convey ideas. Each paragraph of the writing is dedicated to only one idea. The report contains no mechanical errors. The writing is ready to publish.
Comments: _____
_____ **Use of Language:**
The writer creates a structure appropriate to the needs of a specific audience. The writer uses descriptive language that clarifies and enhances ideas. The writer engages the reader. The writer expresses an individual, consistent voice. The writer uses an interesting lead.
Comments: _____
_____ **Organization/Structure:**
The writing is organized and follows the recommended structure for a report. The parts of a report (title, main idea, examples to support the main idea, and summary or conclusion) are present. The report is at least five paragraphs in length.
Comments: _____

Strategies for Assessing Writing in Social Studies (cont.)

Self-Assessment

Background Information

Self-Assessment is a way for students to assess their own work. Students learn to look critically at their own work and analyze it for strengths and weaknesses. A benefit to using Self-Assessment is that students take ownership of the assessment process, which personalizes the learning for them. Some students who are extremely sensitive about receiving feedback may appreciate this method of assessment. Also, teachers can use student reflections as a springboard into developing personal goals for students. Having a personal goal to strive toward will make future writing assignments more meaningful.

Grade Levels

Grades 1–2 (Standard 1.4)
Grades 3–5 (Standard 1.4)
Grades 6–8 (Standard 1.4)

Genres

Expository, Summary, Narrative, Persuasive

Stages of Writing Process

Reflection

Activity

Determine the writing assignment to be used for Self-Assessment. Use the Self-Assessment checklist and personal response survey on pages 194–195 as a guide. Display a copy of the Self-Assessment checklist and survey to see before they begin writing. Tell students that they will be responsible for evaluating their own writing when they have completed the writing assignment.

Encourage students to refer to the checklist and survey throughout the writing process, so that they keep the goals in mind as they work. For students who may be unaccustomed to using self-assessment, consider allowing them to work in pairs to "practice" completing the checklist and survey before they have officially published their work. This may help them look more critically at their own work before the final evaluation. After students have completed their Self-Assessment checklist and survey, take time to conference individually to provide constructive feedback and set goals for the next writing piece. When work begins on the following assignment, ask students to identify one or two elements on the checklist where they would like to improve.

Differentiation

Consider limiting the elements on the checklist for ELLs and students reading and writing below grade level, while still maintaining a focus on using and applying the grade-appropriate social studies content. ELLs will need the checklist adapted to meet their specific needs, so the expectations are appropriate for their current level of language development. Students reading and writing below grade level may focus on one or two elements in each category, so as to not overwhelm them. Challenge gifted students to apply higher-level writing strategies, use more advanced vocabulary, and incorporate more compound, complex, and compound-complex sentence structures. Add to their checklist in areas where they can work on developing their skills, so they are appropriately challenged.

Name: _____

Self-Assessment

Title: _____ **Date:** _____

Topic: _____

Directions: Answer the questions below to self-assess your writing.

1. Capitalization

_____ Did I capitalize the first word of each sentence?

_____ Did I capitalize proper nouns such as names and places?

2. Punctuation

_____ Did I put a ., !, or a ? at the end of each sentence?

_____ Did I use commas in a series?

_____ Did I use commas in dates?

_____ Have I been careful not to use the exclamation point too much?

_____ Have I used quotation marks when I needed them?

3. Handwriting

_____ Did I write neatly?

_____ Are there missing words that need to be added?

_____ Are there extra words that need to be deleted?

4. Spelling

_____ Did I check my spelling?

5. Overall Content

_____ Have I been clear about the topic of my writing?

_____ Is it easy to tell what the main idea is?

_____ Have I used any special words or phrases that add to my writing?

_____ Are there any words or phrases that are confusing?

_____ Have I used an interesting lead?

_____ Have I considered what would make my writing better?

6. Social Studies Content

_____ Did I use the correct social studies terms?

_____ Did I write about the social studies topic accurately?

_____ Did I do adequate research on the social studies topic?

_____ Did I use my own words?

_____ Do I clearly understand the social studies topic I am writing about?

Name: _____

Self-Assessment

Title: _____ **Date:** _____

Topic: _____

I think this writing piece shows that I can...

_____

_____

_____

One thing I learned from writing this is...

_____

_____

_____

I have improved my writing in these areas...

_____

_____

_____

The next time I write, I will...

_____

_____

_____

Did I give my best to this writing assignment? Why or why not?

_____

_____

_____

Strategies for Assessing Writing in Social Studies *(cont.)*

Peer Assessment

Background Information

Peer Assessment is a way for students to practice analyzing the work of others. Students learn to look critically at others' work and analyze it for strengths and weaknesses. They also deepen their understanding of the expectations of each particular writing genre because they must know what a good topic sentence is if they are going to determine if their peers' work has an effective topic sentence. As with Self-Assessment, students take ownership of the assessment process—even though they are not assessing their own work—which personalizes the learning for them. This assessment tool can be used in conjunction with another, such as teacher conference or a traditional rubric. Teachers can also ask students to reflect on what they saw in their partners' work and choose an aspect that they might want to include in their own writing in the future.

Grade Levels

Grades 1–2 (Standard 1.4)
Grades 3–5 (Standard 1.4)
Grades 6–8 (Standard 1.4)

Genres

Expository, Summary, Narrative, Persuasive

Stages of Writing Process

Reflection

Activity

Determine the writing assignment to be used for Peer Assessment. Display a copy of the Peer Assessment (page 197) before students begin writing, and model how to complete it with a sample piece of writing.

This should be a positive process, so provide explicit examples of feedback and constructive criticism so that students are clear on how they are to evaluate a classmates' work. Tell students that they will be responsible for evaluating their peers' writing when they have completed the writing assignment. Encourage students to keep their audience in mind as they work. After all students have completed their writing, distribute copies of the Peer Assessment sheet and assign partners. Have students read their partners' work and add their comments to the assessment. You may wish to collect the Peer Assessment sheets to screen the partners' comments or add your own comments before returning them to students with their written work.

Differentiation

Preteach ELLs how to use the Peer Assessment, as well as some of the language they will need to respond in this activity. Their feedback should be valued as a member of the classroom community. Also consider how to instruct these students' partners about responding to the writing of ELLs, so that their comments are directed toward the expectations of their individual language levels. Adjust their response prompts, if needed. Students reading and writing below grade level may not need differentiation to complete the Peer Assessment form, but their partners may need some guidance on how to respond. Consider altering the checklists for these students' writing to address their levels of proficiency. Have gifted students work in small groups to evaluate their writing based on higher-level prompts, and ask them to provide examples to support their feedback and suggestions.

Name: _____

Peer Assessment

Author's Name: _____ **Date:** _____

Title: _____ **Topic:** _____

Mark an "x" under the appropriate column below:

	Very Much	Somewhat
1. I enjoyed reading this piece of writing.	_____	_____
2. I think this writing is easy to read.	_____	_____
3. The writing is creative.	_____	_____
4. The writing made sense to me.	_____	_____

Finish the following statements as best you can. Remember, your job is to help the writer.

1. One thing I really like about this writing is…

   _____

2. One thing I think the author can improve upon is…

   _____

3. Something I would like to tell the author is…

   _____

4. I think other people that will read this piece will think…

   _____

5. One thing that I can learn from the author and this writing is…

   _____

Strategies for Assessing Writing in Social Studies (cont.)

Teacher Conference

Background Information

Teachers are often frustrated and disappointed when students' writing assignments are turned in off-topic, disorganized, or lacking the proper amount of information. Teacher Conferences allow teachers to maintain consistent communication with their students throughout the writing process. These opportunities, although brief, can keep students on track and give them the scaffolds and suggestions they need to create a better piece of writing. It is important for teachers to also take the time in these conferences to ask questions of students, and listen to what challenges they might be facing, so students feel that the conferences are less evaluative and more cooperative.

Grade Levels

Grades 1–2 (Standard 1.4)
Grades 3–5 (Standard 1.4)
Grades 6–8 (Standard 1.4)

Genres

Expository, Summary, Narrative, Persuasive

Stages of Writing Process

Reflection

Activity

Determine the writing assignment to be used for Teacher Conferences. Display a copy of the Teacher Conference form (page 199) for students to see before they begin writing. Tell students that they will be meeting with you at each phase of the writing process to discuss their writing, share concerns, ask for suggestions, and receive feedback.

Students should keep their copy of the form with them as they write. Encourage them to refer to the form throughout the writing process, so they keep the goals of each phase in mind as they work. As you take students through each phase of the writing process, take time to conference individually to provide constructive feedback and set goals for the next phase. When their writing assignment is complete, be sure to add clear, explicit feedback, so students have a clear understanding of the strengths and weaknesses of their work. When students begin the next assignment, ask them to identify one or two elements on the checklist where they would like to improve.

Differentiation

Consider limiting the elements on the checklist for ELLs and students reading and writing below grade level, while still maintaining a focus of using and applying the grade-appropriate social studies content. ELLs will need the checklist adapted to meet their specific needs, so the expectations are appropriate for their current level of language development. Students reading and writing below grade level may focus on one or two elements in each category, so as to not overwhelm them. Gifted students should be challenged to apply higher-level writing strategies, use more advanced vocabulary, and incorporate more compound, complex, and compound-complex sentence structures. Add to their checklist in areas where they can work on developing their skills, so they are appropriately challenged.

Name: _____

Teacher Conference

Title: _____ **Date:** _____

Topic: _____

	Needs Work	Good	Excellent
Brainstorming			
The writing is well thought out.	_____	_____	_____
The writing is easy to follow.	_____	_____	_____
The writing is creative and interesting.	_____	_____	_____
Drafting			
The writing is organized.	_____	_____	_____
The writing uses the correct format.	_____	_____	_____
The writing is complete.	_____	_____	_____
Editing and Revising			
The writing has complete sentences.	_____	_____	_____
The writing uses correct punctuation.	_____	_____	_____
The writing uses capitalization correctly.	_____	_____	_____
The writing uses correct spelling.	_____	_____	_____
The writing uses transition words.	_____	_____	_____
Publishing			
The writing is written or typed neatly.	_____	_____	_____
The writing has a capitalized title.	_____	_____	_____
The writing has been illustrated, if needed.	_____	_____	_____

Teacher Comments

Your writing is very good in these ways: _____

_____

_____

Your writing could be made better by doing these things: _____

_____

_____

Works Cited

Adams, M. 1990. *Beginning to read: Thinking and learning about print.* Urbana-Champaign, IL: University of Illinois, Reading Research and Education Center.

Anderson, R., and P. Freebody. 1985. Vocabulary knowledge. In *Theoretical models and processes of reading.* 3rd ed. Ed. H. Singer and R. B. Ruddell, 343–371. Newark, DE: International Reading Association.

Angelo, T. A., and K. P. Cross. 1993. *Classroom assessment techniques: A handbook for college teachers.* 2nd ed. San Francisco: Jossey-Bass.

Atwell, N. 1984. Writing and reading literature from the inside out. *Language Arts* 61 (3): 240–252.

Barr, M. A., and M. K. Healy. 1988. School and university articulation: Different contexts for writing across the curriculum. *New Directions for Teaching and Learning* 36 (Winter): 43–53.

Bean, J. 1996. Helping students read difficult texts. In *Engaging ideas: The professor's guide to integrating writing, critical thinking, and active learning in the classroom,* 133–147. San Francisco: Jossey-Bass.

Becker, W. C. 1977. Teaching reading and language to the disadvantaged—What we have learned from field research. *Harvard Educational Review* 47 (4): 518–543.

Blackburn, E. 1982. The rhythm of writing development. In *Understanding writing: Ways of observing, learning, and teaching,* ed. N. Atwell and T. Newkirk. Chelmsford, MA: Northeast Regional Exchange.

Boutwell, M. 1983. Reading and writing: A reciprocal agreement. *Language Arts* 60 (6): 723–730.

Bringle, R., and J. Hatcher. 1996. Reflection activities for the college classroom. Paper presented at the National Gathering on June 21.

Britton, J., T. Burgess, N. Martin, A. McLeod, and H. Rosen. 1975. *The development of writing abilities,* 11-18. New York: Macmillan Education.

Brozo, W., and M. Simpson. 2003. *Readers, teachers, learners: Expanding literacy across the content areas.* 4th ed. Upper Saddle River, NJ: Merrill.

Calkins, L. 1983. *Lessons from a child.* Portsmouth, NH: Heinemann.

Carey-Webb, A. 2001. *Literature and lives: A response-based, cultural studies approach to teaching English.* Urbana, IL: NCTE.

Chamot, A. U., and J. M. O'Malley. 1994. *The CALLA handbook.* Reading, MA: Addison-Wesley.

Christen, W. L., and T. J. Murphy. 1991. Increasing comprehension by activating prior knowledge. ERIC Digest. Bloomington, IN: ERIC Clearinghouse on Reading, English, and Communication.

Works Cited *(cont.)*

Cohen, A. D. 1994. *Assessing language ability in the classroom.* 2nd ed. Boston: Heinle and Heinle.

Corona, C., S. Spangenberger, and I. Venet. 1998. Improving student writing through a language rich environment. M.A. Action Research Project, St. Xavier University and IRI/Skylight, 61 pages.

Dechant, E. 1991. *Understanding and teaching reading: An interactive model.* Hillsdale, NJ: Lawrence Erlbaum.

Duke, N. K., and P. D. Pearson. 2001. Developing comprehension in the primary grades. A Presentation to the International Reading Association.

Eanet, M. G., and A. V. Manzo. 1976. REAP—A strategy for improving reading/writing/study skills. *Journal of Reading* 19 (8): 647–652.

Elbow, Peter. 1973. *Writing without teachers.* New York: Oxford UP.

Emig, J. 1977. Writing as a mode of learning. *College Composition and Communication* 28 (2): 122–128.

Feuer, M. J., and K. Fulton. 1993. The many faces of performance assessment. *Phi Delta Kappan* 74 (6): 478.

Fisher, D., and N. Frey. 2004. *Improving adolescent literacy: Strategies at work.* Upper Saddle River, NJ: Pearson Education.

Fisher, D., and G. Ivey. 2005. Literacy and language as learning in content area classes: A departure from "every teacher a teacher of reading." *Action in Teacher Education* 27 (2): 3–11.

Flores, A., and C. Brittain. 2003. Writing to reflect in a mathematics methods course. *Teaching Children Mathematics* 10 (2): 112–118.

Frayer, D. A., W. C. Frederick, and H. J. Klausmeier. 1969. In *A word is a word . . . or is it?*, ed. M. F. Graves. New York: Scholastic, 1985.

Fulwiler, T. 1980. Journals across the disciplines. *English Journal* 69 (12): 14.

Gahn, S. M. 1989. A practical guide for teaching and writing in the content areas. *Journal of Reading* 32 (6): 525–531.

Gere, A., ed. 1985. *Roots in the sawdust: Writing to learn across the discipline.* Urbana, IL: National Council of Teachers of English.

Graves, D. H. 1983. *Writing: Teachers and children at work.* Portsmouth, NH: Heinemann.

Graves, D., and J. Hansen. 1983. The author's chair. *Language Arts* 60 (2): 176–83.

Greenberg, J., and C. Rath. 1985. Empowering students through writing. *Educational Leadership* 42 (5): 10–13.

Works Cited (cont.)

Haggard, M. R. 1986. The vocabulary self-collection strategy: An active approach to word learning. In *Reading in the content areas: Improving classroom instruction.* 2nd ed. Ed. E. K. Dishner, 179–183. Dubuque, IA: Kendall/Hunt.

Haggard, M. R. 1986. The vocabulary self-collection strategy: Using student interest and world knowledge to enhance vocabulary growth. *Journal of Reading* 29 (7): 634–642.

Hamilton-Wieler, S. 1988. Awkward compromises and eloquent achievements. *English Education* 21 (3): 152–169.

Hamp-Lyons, E. 1983. Developing a course to teach extensive reading skills to university-bound ESL learners. *System* 11 (3): 303–312.

Harste, J. C., K. G. Short, and C. Burke. 1988. *Creating classrooms for authors: The reading-writing connection.* Portsmouth, NH: Heinemann.

Hefflin, B., and D. Hartman. 2002. Using writing to improve comprehension: A review of the writing-to-reading research. In *Improving comprehension instruction: Rethinking research, theory, and classroom practice,* ed. C. C. Block, L. B. Gambrell, and M. Pressley, 199–228. San Francisco: Jossey-Bass.

Herman, J. L., P. R. Aschbacher, and L. Winters. 1992. *A practical guide to alternative assessment.* Alexandria, VA: ASCD, Hodgson & Bohning.

Hightshue, D., et al. 1988. Writing in junior and senior high schools. *Phi Delta Kappan* 69 (10): 725–728.

Hoyt, J. E. 1999. Remedial education and student attrition. *Community College Review* 27 (2): 51–73.

Huba, M. E., and J. E. Freed. 2000. Using rubrics to provide feedback to students. In *Learner-centered assessment on college campuses,* 151–200. Needham Heights, MA: Allyn & Bacon.

Jones, B. F., A. S. Palincsar, D. S. Ogle, and E. G. Carr. 1987. *Strategic teaching and learning: Cognitive instruction in the content areas.* Alexandria, VA: ASCD, Jossey-Bass.

Laflamme, J. G. 1997. The effect of multiple exposure vocabulary method and the target reading/writing strategy on test scores. *Journal of Adolescent & Adult Literacy* 40 (5): 372–384.

Lenski, S. D., M. A. Wham, and J. L. Johns. 1999. *Reading & learning strategies for middle & high school students.* Dubuque, IA: Kendall/Hunt.

Lesley, M. 2005. Looking for critical literacy with postbaccalaureate content area literacy students. *Journal of Adolescent & Adult Literacy* 48 (4): 320–334.

Works Cited (cont.)

Marzano, R. J., D. Pickering, and J. McTighe. 1993. *Assessing student outcomes: Performance assessment using the dimensions of learning model.* Alexandria, VA: Association for Supervision and Curriculum Development.

Moore, D. W., and S. A. Moore. 1986. Possible sentences. In *Reading in the content areas: Improving classroom instruction.* 2nd edition. Ed. E. K. Dishner, T. W. Bean, J. E. Readence, and D. W. Moore. Dubuque, IA: Kendall/Hunt.

Moore, D., S. Moore, P. Cunningham, and J. Cunningham. 1994. *Developing readers and writers in the content areas: K–12.* 2nd ed. White Plains, NY: Longman.

Nagy, W. E., and J. A. Scott. 2000. Vocabulary processes. In *Handbook of reading research*, ed. M. L. Kamil, P. B. Mosenthal, P. D. Pearson, and R. Barr, 269–284. Mahwah, NJ: Lawrence Erlbaum Associates.

National Research Council. 1996. National science education standards. Washington, DC: National Academy Press.

O'Brien, D. G., and R. A. Stewart. 1990. Preservice teachers' perspectives on why every teacher is not a teacher of reading: A qualitative analysis. *Journal of Reading Behavior* 22 (2): 101–129.

O'Brien, D. G., R. A. Stewart, and E. Moje. 1995. Why content literacy is difficult to infuse into the secondary school: Complexities of curriculum, pedagogy, and school culture. *Reading Research Quarterly* 30 (3): 442–463.

Ogle, D. M. 1986. KWL: A teaching model that develops active reading of expository text. *Reading Teacher* 39 (6): 564–70.

Palmatier, R. 1973. A note taking system for learning. *Journal of Reading* 17 (1): 36–39.

Pauk, W. 1988. *A user's guide to college: Making notes and taking tests.* Lincolnwood, IL: Jamestown Publishers.

Perkins, K. 1983. On the use of composition scoring techniques, objective measures, and objective tests to evaluate ESL writing ability. *TESOL Quarterly* 17 (4): 651–671.

Perkins D. N., and G. Salomon. 1988. Teaching for transfer. *Educational Leadership* 46 (1): 22–32.

Pinnell, G. S. 1988 (January). Success of children at risk in a program that combines writing and reading. *Technical Report No. 417.* Reading and Writing Connections.

Pressley, M. 1990. *Cognitive strategy instruction that really improves children's academic performance.* Cambridge, MA: Brookline Books.

Readance, J. E., T. W. Bean, and R. S. Baldwin. 1981. *Content area literacy: An integrated approach.* Dubuque, IA: Kendall Hunt Publishing.

Resnick, L., and L. Klopfer, eds. 1989. *Toward the thinking curriculum: Current cognitive research.* Alexandria, VA: Association for Supervision and Curriculum Development.

Works Cited *(cont.)*

Ryder, R., and M. Graves. 2003. *Reading and learning in content areas.* 3rd ed. New York: John Wiley & Sons, Inc.

Santa, C. M., L. Havens, and S. Harrison. 1996. Teaching secondary science through reading, writing, studying, and problem solving. In *Content area reading and learning instructional strategies*, ed. D. Lapp, J. Flood, and N. Farnan, 165–179. Needham Heights, MA: Allyn & Bacon.

Schwartz, R., and T. Raphael. 1985. Concept of definition: A key to improving students' vocabulary. *The Reading Teacher* 39 (2): 198–205.

Self, J., ed. 1987. *Plain talk about learning and writing across the curriculum.* Richmond, VA: Virginia Department of Education.

Sloan, M. 1996. Encouraging young students to use interesting words in their writing. *The Reading Teacher* 50 (3): 268–269.

Smith, C. C., and T. W. Bean. 1980. The guided writing procedure: Integrating content reading and writing improvement. *Reading World* 19 (3): 290–294.

Sorenson, S. 1989. *Webster's new world high school writer's handbook: A complete guide for writing across the curriculum.* Englewood Cliffs, NJ: Prentice Hall.

Staton, J. 1980. Writing and counseling: Using a dialogue journal. *Language Arts* 57 (5): 514–518.

Steffens, H. 1988. The value and difficulties of teaching the history of science and technology in secondary schools. Paper presented at the Annual Meeting of the American Historical Association. Cincinnati, OH: 17p. ED 306 182.

Taba, H. 1967. *Teacher's handbook for elementary social studies.* Palo Alto, CA: Addison-Wesley.

Tierney, R., R. Caplan, L. Ehri, M. K. Healy, and M. Hurdlow. 1989. Writing and reading working together. In *Collaboration through writing and reading*, ed. A. H. Dyson, 169–209. Urbana, IL: National Council of Teachers of English.

Vacca, R. T., and J. L. Vacca. 2005. *Content area reading: Literacy and learning across the curriculum.* 8th ed. Boston: Allyn & Bacon.

Venn, J. 1880. On the diagrammatic and mechanical representation of propositions and reasonings. *Philosophical Magazine and Journal of Science* 9 (59): 1–18.

Walker, A. 1988. Writing-across-the-curriculum: The second decade. *English Quarterly* 21 (2): 93–103.

Weinstein, C. E., and R. M. Mayer. 1986. The teaching of learning strategies. In *Handbook of research on teaching and learning*, ed. M. Whitrock, 315–327. New York: MacMillan.

Works Cited *(cont.)*

West, C. K., J. A. Farmer, and P. M. Wolff. 1991. *Instructional design: Implications from cognitive science.* Englewood Cliffs, NJ: Prentice Hall.

Widmayer, S., E. Collins, H. Gray, L. Miller, and G. Rossen. 2004. Technology that reaches and teaches every student. TESOL Pre-Convention Institute.

Willis, S. 1992. Linking the disciplines. *ASCD Update* 34 (2): 1, 6.

Winchester School District, MA. 1987. *Winchester High School Excellence in Education Grant: Reading and Writing Across the Curriculum Final Report.* Washington: Office of Educational Research and Improvement. ED 305 589.

Wood, K. 1984. Probable passage: A writing strategy. *The Reading Teacher* 37 (6): 496–499.

Worsley, D., and B. Mayer. 1989. *The art of science writing.* New York: Teachers and Writers Collaborative.

Yinger, R. 1985. Journal writing as a learning tool. *Volta Review* 87 (5): 21–33.

References for Further Reading

Cunningham, J. W., P. M. Cunningham, and S. V. Arthur. 1981. *Middle and secondary school reading.* New York: Longman.

Fulwiler, T. 1982. Writing: An act of cognition. In *Teaching writing in all disciplines,* ed. C. W. Griffin, 15–23. San Fransisco: Jossey-Bass.

Gagne, E. D., C. W. Yekovich, and F. R. Yekovich. 1993. *The cognitive psychology of school learning.* New York: Addison-Wesley.

McGinley, W., and P. Denner. 1987. Story impressions: A prereading/writing activity. *The Journal of Reading* 31 (3): 248–253.

McNeil, J. 1990. *The essentials of teaching.* Farmington Hills, MI: Macmillan.

O'Malley, J. M., and A. U. Charmot. 1990. *Learning strategies in second language acquisition.* Cambridge: Cambridge University Press.

Pearson, P. D., R. Barr, M. L. Kamil, and P. Mosenthal, eds. 1984. *Handbook of reading research.* New York: Longman, Inc.

Pearson, P. D., and L. Fielding. 1991. Comprehension instruction. In vol. 2 of *Handbook of reading research,* ed. R. Barr, M. L. Kamil, P. B. Mosenthal, and P. D. Pearson, 815–860. White Plains, NY: Longman.

Pearson, P. D., and D. Johnson. 1978. *Teaching reading comprehension.* New York: Holt, Rinehart, and Winston.

Poplin, M. S. 1988. Holistic/constructivist principles of the teaching learning process: Implications for the field of learning disabilities. *Journal of Learning Disabilities* 21 (7): 401–416.

Notes

Notes